GCSE OCR Additional Applied Science The Workbook

This book is for anyone doing **GCSE OCR Additional Applied Science** at foundation level.

GCSE Science is all about **understanding how science works**. And not only that — understanding it well enough to be able to **question** what you hear on TV and read in the papers.

But you can't do that without a fair chunk of **background knowledge**. Hmm, tricky.

This book is full of **tricky questions**... each one designed to make you sweat — because that's the only way you'll get any **better**.

There are questions to see **what facts** you know. There are questions to see how well you can **apply those facts**. And there are questions to see how well you understand the role of **scientists** in the **real world**.

It's also got some daft bits in to try and make the whole experience at least vaguely entertaining for you.

What CGP is all about

Our sole aim here at CGP is to produce the highest quality books — carefully written, immaculately presented and dangerously close to being funny.

Then we work our socks off to get them out to you — at the cheapest possible prices.

Contents

Unit 1: Topic 1 — Sport and Fitness

Unit 1: Topic 2 — Health Care

Unit 1: Topic 3 — Protecting the Environment

Unit 1: Topic 4 — Protecting the Public

Published by CGP

Editors:
Charlotte Burrows, Helena Hayes, Rosie McCurrie, Rachael Rogers, Hayley Thompson.

Contributors:
Mark Edwards, Andy Rankin.

ISBN: 978 1 84762 882 4

With thanks to Janet Cruse-Sawyer and Jamie Sinclair for the proofreading.

With thanks to Anna Lupton for the copyright research.

With thanks to Eye of Science/Science Photo Library for permission to reproduce the photograph on page 48.

Pages 100, 101 and 122 contain public sector information published by the Health and Safety Executive and licensed under the Open Government Licence v1.0.
http://www.nationalarchives.gov.uk/doc/open-government-licence/

Every effort has been made to locate copyright holders and obtain permission to reproduce sources. For those sources where it has been difficult to trace the originator of the work, we would be grateful for information. If any copyright holder would like us to make an amendment to the acknowledgements, please notify us and we will gladly update the book at the next reprint.
Thank you.

Groovy website: www.cgpbooks.co.uk

Printed by Elanders Ltd, Newcastle upon Tyne.
Jolly bits of clipart from CorelDRAW®
Based on the classic CGP style created by Richard Parsons.

Fitness Facilities

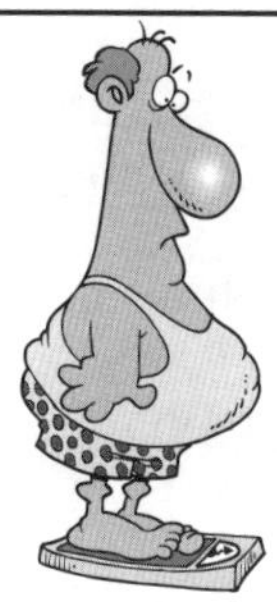

Q1 After spending the summer eating pies, Richard has decided to **get fit**.

a) Suggest a local indoor facility he could visit to improve his fitness.

....

b) Which of the following would you expect to find at a fitness facility?
Circle the correct answer(s).

weights   X-ray machines   treadmills   doctors   aerobics classes

c) There are several fitness facilities in the town where Richard lives.
Suggest **two** ways in which this could have a **positive impact** on the local community.

1. ....

....

2. ....

....

Q2 Rosemary works as a **personal trainer** at a gym.

a) Complete the following paragraph using words from the box.

monitoring	body	assess	programme	improve

Personal trainers work with individual people to .... their fitness.
They must have a good understanding of how the .... works.
They must be able to carry out basic tests to .... a person's fitness.
They then use this information to develop and modify a fitness ....,
as well as regularly .... their client's fitness.

b) Rosemary must follow health and safety regulations as part of her job.
Which of the following describes a **health and safety regulation** that Rosemary must follow?
Tick **one** box.

☐ She must be able to advise clients on what a good diet is.

☐ She must be able to show clients how to carry out exercises correctly, to prevent injuries.

☐ She must have knowledge of how muscles work in the body.

Baseline Assessment

Q1 Olivia is a **fitness coach**. Whenever she gets a new client, she carries out a **baseline assessment**. As part of this assessment, Olivia asks her client about his or her **lifestyle**, **health** and **fitness**.

a) Draw lines to connect each of the words on the left to its description.

LIFESTYLE	A measure of how well you can perform physical tasks.
HEALTH	The way a person lives their life.
FITNESS	A state of mental, physical and social well-being.

b) Complete the table below to say whether each of the following relates to part of a person's lifestyle, health or fitness. The first one has been done for you.

~~pregnancy~~ stamina cigarettes smoked stress levels previous injuries strength medications taken operations had

Lifestyle	Health	Fitness
	pregnancy	

Q2 Paul is worried that his **lifestyle** is affecting his **fitness**. Tick the boxes to show whether the following statements are **true** or **false**.

		True	False
a)	Drinking too much alcohol can affect your fitness.	☐	☐
b)	A person's diet has no effect on their fitness.	☐	☐
c)	A person's stamina can be improved by doing more exercise.	☐	☐
d)	Stress can affect a person's ability to carry out physical tasks.	☐	☐

Top Tips: Describing the difference between lifestyle, health and fitness can be tricky — but make sure you can do it. Make sure you know how lifestyle factors can affect fitness too. Eating lots of biscuits has actually improved my fitness — the walk to the biscuit barrel does me the world of good.

Basic Tests

Q1 Katie has just joined a **women's football club**. Before she begins training she is given a few **basic tests** by the club doctor.

a) The doctor takes Katie's **temperature**, which she finds to be 37.3 °C.
The doctor tells Katie that a normal core body temperature is between **36.5 and 37 °C**.

i) Which statement best describes Katie's temperature? Tick the box next to the correct statement.

☐ Katie's temperature is too low.

☐ Katie's temperature is too high.

☐ It's impossible to know if Katie's temperature is too high or low because body temperature varies greatly.

ii) Give **one** reason why someone's body temperature might be higher than average.

....

iii) Give **three** types of thermometer that the doctor may have used to check Katie's temperature.

1. ....

2. ....

3. ....

b) The doctor tells Katie that she is about to use a piece of equipment called a **sphygmomanometer**.
What does a sphygmomanometer measure?

....

Q2 Tom's aerobics instructor tells his aerobics class that a healthy resting pulse rate for an adult is **60-100** beats per minute. The class decide to measure their **pulse rates** while at rest. The results for four of the class members are shown below.

Person	Pulse rate (beats per minute)
Tom	55
Steven	75
Alice	110
Mary	80

a) Which **two** people have a pulse rate within the healthy range for an adult?

....

....

b) Suggest **one** reason why someone's pulse rate might be high.

....

....

Basic Tests

Q3 Duncan is **recovering** from a leg injury. As part of his recovery, he is advised to take part in a **specialist training programme**. Before Duncan begins the programme, his **fitness** is assessed by his instructor.

a) During the assessment, the instructor measures Duncan's pulse rate at rest. Tick the boxes to show whether these statements about taking someone's pulse rate are **true** or **false**.

	True	False
i) Pulse rates are measured using a thermometer.	☐	☐
ii) You need a stopwatch or a watch with a second hand to take an accurate pulse rate.	☐	☐
iii) Pulse rate is usually measured at an artery in the shoulder.	☐	☐

b) When measuring Duncan's pulse rate, the instructor counts 33 pulses in 30 seconds. Calculate Duncan's pulse rate in beats per minute (bpm).

....

....

c) Duncan also has his **blood pressure** measured as part of the assessment.

i) Which of the following can be used to measure blood pressure? Tick **one** box.

a blood test	☐	a stopwatch	☐
a thermometer	☐	an electronic sensor	☐

ii) Duncan is given a leaflet about blood pressure. The leaflet contains the following information.

> **A blood pressure reading of:**
> - **less than 90/60 mmHg is low.**
> - **between 90/60 and 120/80 mmHG is normal and healthy.**
> - **between 120/80 and 140/90 mmHG is normal, but slightly high.**
> - **more than 140/90 mmHG is high.**

Duncan's reading was 134/80 mmHg. Is his blood pressure normal? Explain your answer.

....

....

Top Tips: These two pages might be called 'Basic Tests', but don't make the mistake of thinking your exam will be basic — those pesky examiners really like to test you. If you really want to impress, learn to spell that sphygo.. sphygomoma-wotsit... you know the one I mean.

More Basic Tests

Q1 A personal trainer wants to find out which of his clients has the shortest **'recovery' time**. This is the time it takes for your pulse rate to **return to normal** after exercise. He measures each client's **pulse rate**, then asks them to **run** for 2 minutes. After they've finished running, he measures their pulse rate at 15 second intervals until it has returned to normal.

To the right is a sketch of his results.

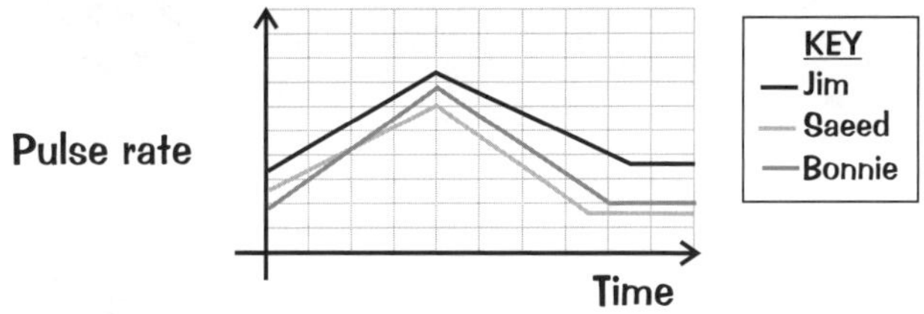

a) Which of the clients has the **shortest** recovery time?

....

b) What does someone's recovery time tell you about their level of **aerobic fitness**?

....

....

....

Q2 Louise and Charlotte have their **body mass** measured when they join a gym. Louise has a mass of 54 kg and Charlotte has a mass of 73 kg.

a) What equipment can be used to measure body mass?

....

b) Tick the box to show which statement is **true**.

Louise is a normal weight but Charlotte is overweight. ☐

Louise is underweight but Charlotte is a normal weight. ☐

You cannot tell if Louise and Charlotte are overweight or underweight without more information. ☐

c) Louise and Charlotte want to calculate their body mass index (BMI). To calculate their BMI they need to know their **height** as well as their mass.

i) What equipment could they use to measure their height?

....

ii) Louise calculates her body mass index (BMI) as **17.7**. Charlotte's is **26.7**. Using the table on the right, what advice would be given to each of them if they wanted to be a healthy weight?

BMI	Condition
<18.5	underweight
18.5 - 24.9	healthy weight
25 - 29.9	overweight
>30	obese

Louise: ....

Charlotte: ....

The Breathing System

Q1 Paul competes in the 400 m relay but has recently noticed he's getting out of breath quicker than usual. His coach is worried he has a **chest infection** and sends him to see his doctor.

a) Label the diagram of the breathing system.

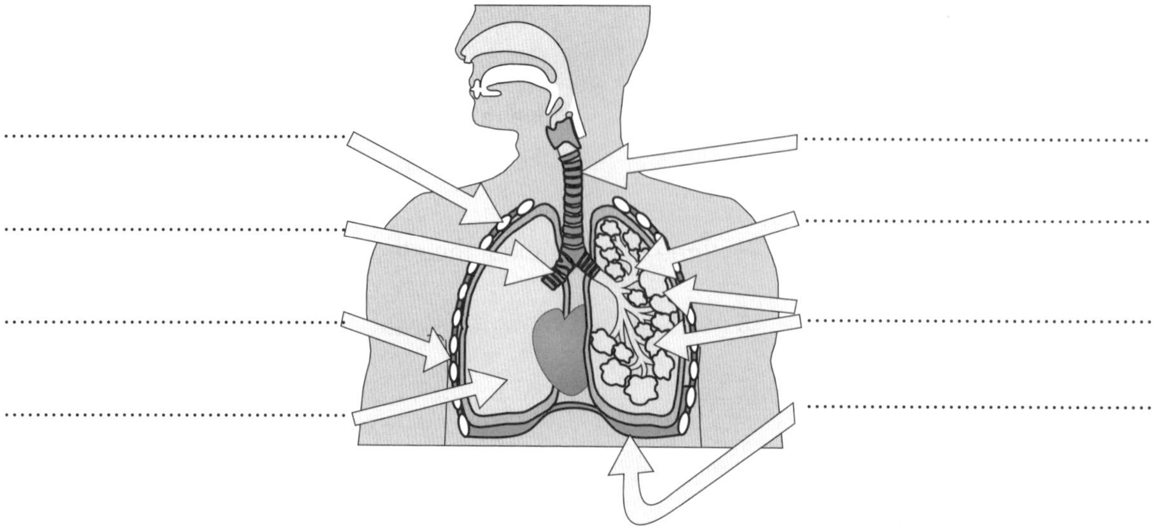

b) Draw lines to connect each part of the breathing system to its description.

alveoli	Tubes that transport gases into and out of the lungs.
bronchi	Tiny air sacs that provide a large surface area for gas exchange.
diaphragm	Muscle below the lungs that contracts and relaxes to help with breathing.
intercostal muscles	A set of muscles that raise and lower the ribs to help with breathing.
lungs	Bones that protect the heart and lungs and help with breathing.
ribs	Pipe that connects the mouth and nose to the lungs.
trachea	Organs for the exchange of oxygen and carbon dioxide.

c) Circle the correct word(s) in each pair to complete the following sentences.

i) When Paul breathes in, his intercostal muscles and diaphragm **contract** / **relax**. This moves the ribcage **up and out** / **down and in**, which **increases** / **decreases** the volume of the lungs, causing air to enter.

ii) To breathe out, the muscles in Paul's chest **contract** / **relax**. This **increases** / **decreases** the pressure in his lungs, which forces air out.

Top Tips: Don't forget, air moves in and out of the lungs because the intercostal muscles and diaphragm contract and relax to change the pressure — air doesn't just move in and out on its own.

The Blood and Blood Vessels

Q1 By training hard, athletes can improve the **oxygen supply** to their muscles. Oxygen is transported round the body in the **blood**.

a) Which type of blood cell transports oxygen?

....

b) Name **three** components of blood.

1. ....

2. ....

3. ....

c) Blood is carried around the body in **blood vessels**, such as **veins**.

Complete the following paragraph about veins, using words from the box.

higher	fowardflow	valves	thicker	backflow	thinner	lower	from	to

Veins have .... walls than arteries because they transport blood at .... pressure. Veins transport blood .... the heart, often against the flow of gravity, so they have .... to stop the blood flowing the wrong way. Blood flowing the wrong way is called ....

Q2 Huang falls off his bike during a race and has a **cut** that won't stop **bleeding**. The doctor tells Huang that he has injured an **artery**.

a) i) What is the function of arteries? ....

ii) Give **one** way that the structure of an artery is specialised for this function.

....

b) Huang also has bruises on his knees where capillaries have been broken. Capillaries break easily because they have very thin walls.

Why is it useful for capillaries to have such thin walls?

....

....

The Heart and Respiration

Q1 Padma is hoping to compete in the **triathlon** in the next Olympics.
She asks her coach to tell her about how the **heart pumps blood** around the body.

a) **i)** Label the diagram of the heart below, using words from the box.

right atrium	left ventricle	right ventricle	left atrium

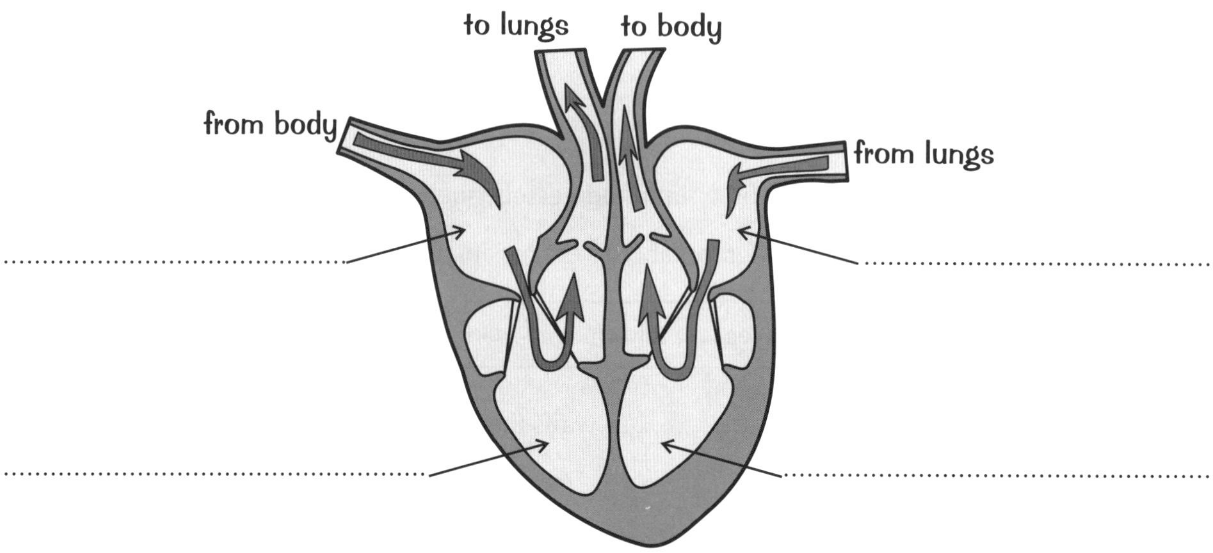

ii) Circle **two valves** on the diagram.

b) The statements below describe the flow of blood **from the body** through the heart and lungs. Number the boxes to put the statements in the correct order. The first one has been done for you.

☐ Blood passes into the left ventricle, which pumps it out and round the whole body.

☐ Blood flows through a valve into the right ventricle.

☐ Blood leaves the heart and flows to the lungs.

1 Deoxygenated blood from the body enters the right atrium.

☐ Oxygenated blood from the lungs flows into the left atrium.

The Heart and Respiration

Q2 **100 m sprinters** run very fast for a short period of time. **Distance runners** run for much longer at a slower pace. Training exercises are classed as '**aerobic**' or '**anaerobic**', depending on which kind of **respiration** is mostly used. 100 m sprinters do more **anaerobic** training than distance runners.

a) Circle the correct word equation for **aerobic respiration**.

glucose + oxygen → carbon dioxide + water (+ energy)

protein + oxygen → carbon dioxide + water (+ energy)

glucose + carbon dioxide → oxygen + water (+ energy)

b) What does the term '**aerobic**' in aerobic respiration mean?

....

c) Tick the correct boxes to show whether the sentences about aerobic respiration are **true** or **false**.

	True	False
i) Aerobic respiration releases energy.	☐	☐
ii) Respiration usually releases energy from protein.	☐	☐
iii) Respiration takes place in every cell in your body.	☐	☐
iv) Oxygen is a waste product from aerobic respiration.	☐	☐
v) The waste products of aerobic respiration are carried away from cells by the blood.	☐	☐

d) Use some of the words given below to complete the word equation for **anaerobic respiration**.

carbon dioxide **oxygen** **lactic acid** **water** **glucose** **energy**

Anaerobic: .... → .... (+ ....)

e) Complete the following sentences about anaerobic respiration by circling the correct word(s) from each pair.

i) Anaerobic respiration is respiration **with** / **without** oxygen.

ii) In anaerobic respiration, **glucose** / **carbon dioxide** is partially broken down.

iii) The waste product from anaerobic respiration is **carbon dioxide** / **lactic acid**.

iv) The waste product from anaerobic respiration is carried away from the cells **by blood** / **in air**.

The Kidneys

Q1 **Sports scientists** studied the effect of **water intake** on **urine production**. Groups of people drank a set volume of water over **24 hours**, and the volume of **urine** they produced was recorded.

Their results are shown on the graph opposite.

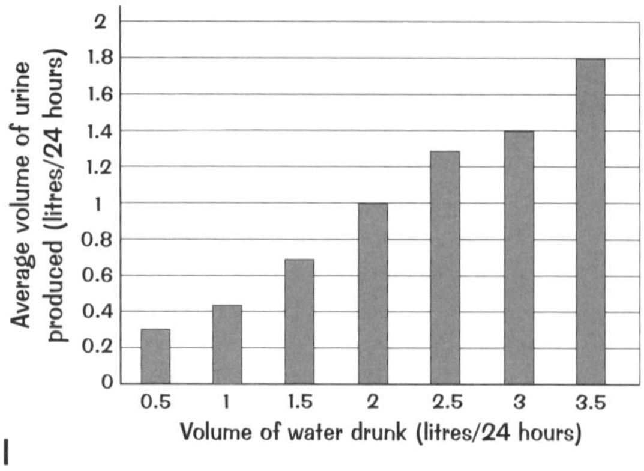

a) What happened to the **volume of urine** produced as the volume of water drunk increased? Circle the correct answer.

it increased **it stayed the same** **it decreased**

b) How much water would you expect the group that produced the **palest** urine to have drunk? Circle the correct answer.

0.5 l **1 l** **1.5 l** **2 l** **2.5 l** **3 l** **3.5 l**

c) Which organ in the body produces urine? Circle the correct answer.

bladder **kidney** **gall bladder** **sphincter** **liver**

d) Give **two** ways, other than in urine, in which water is **lost** from the body.

1. ....

2. ....

e) Give **one** way, other than through drink, in which water is **gained** by the body.

....

Q2 Milly is an **athlete**. She has regular **blood tests** to check her general health.

a) The tests measure the amount of **urea** in Milly's blood.

i) What is urea? ....

ii) Why is it important that it is removed from the blood?

....

b) The test also measures the concentration of **ions** in Milly's blood.

i) Why is it dangerous to have a very high or a very low ion content in the body?

....

....

ii) Give **two** ways in which ions are removed from the body.

1. ....

2. ....

Joints

Q1 Caroline has hurt her leg playing **rounders**. A **physiotherapist** shows her a diagram of the **calf muscle** to help explain her injury.

Tick the boxes to show whether the following statements are **true** or **false**.

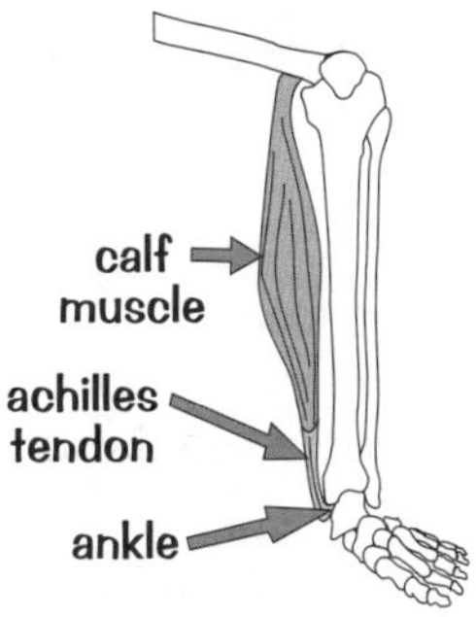

	True	False
a) Caroline's calf muscle is attached to her bones by tendons.	☐	☐
b) When a tendon contracts it moves the calf muscle.	☐	☐
c) When the calf muscle contracts it pulls on the bone.	☐	☐
d) The bones in Caroline's knee are held together by ligaments.	☐	☐
e) Ligaments are very strong and quite elastic.	☐	☐

Q2 Bo was once a prize-winning **weightlifter**. He is now doing a Foundation Degree in Sports Coaching. To get his qualification he must learn all about the **joints** in the body and how they work. One of the joints he must learn about is the **knee**.

a) Label the diagram of the knee below, using words from the box. You may use some of the words more than once.

cartilage	ligament	tendon	muscle	bone

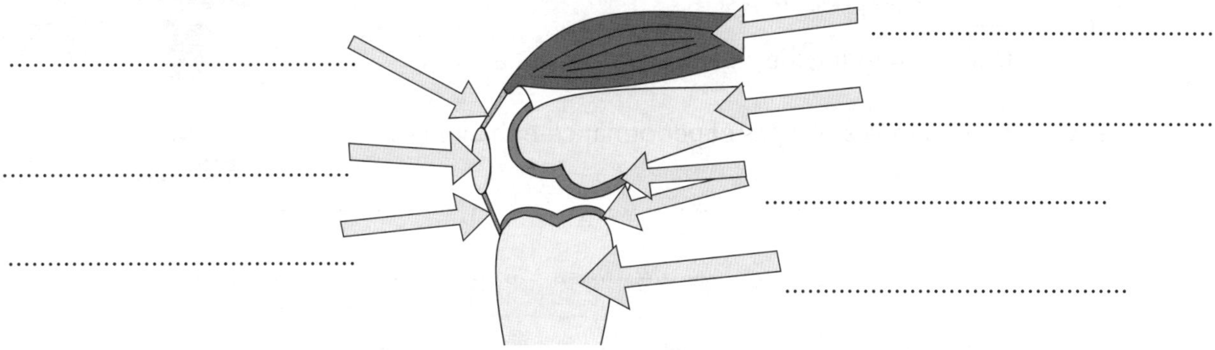

b) Explain the role of each of the following parts of a joint:

Cartilage: ....

....

Muscles: ....

....

Top Tips: You need to be able to describe the general structure of a joint and explain what role each of the different parts plays. They're all important. And for the record, it's probably best you don't have a favourite part — they're renowned for getting very jealous. Cartilage in particular.

Monitoring and Improving Performance

Q1 Daniel is a **100 m sprinter**.

a) Three times a week, Daniel's coach times how long it takes him to run 100 m.

i) In one training session, Daniel runs 100 m in 12.5 seconds. Calculate his **speed**.

Speed = distance ÷ time

....

.... m/s

ii) Suggest why Daniel's coach records how long it takes him to run 100 m on a regular basis.

....

....

....

b) Daniel is regularly tested for performance-enhancing drug use.

i) Which of the following methods could be used to detect whether Daniel has taken any drugs? Tick **one** box.

- ☐ Urine test
- ☐ Blood pressure test
- ☐ Monitoring the athlete's performance

ii) Give **two** examples of types of performance-enhancing drugs.

1. ....

2. ....

Q2 Anna's personal trainer has designed a training programme for her to improve her **fitness**. Part of the training programme is shown below.

> Lift a 2 kg weight for 10 repetitions (on each arm) twice a week.

a) What type of exercise is this? Tick **one** box.

Aerobic exercise ☐ Muscle-building exercise ☐

b) Anna's personal trainer thinks she's doing well with her training programme and decides to modify it to improve her fitness further. Suggest **two** changes the personal trainer might make to the part of the plan shown above.

1. ....

2. ....

Physiotherapists

Q1 The NHS has produced a leaflet explaining the role of a **physiotherapist**. The following passage is taken from the leaflet. **Fill in the gaps** using the words in the box. Use each word only once.

test **exercises** **assess** **symptoms** **treatments**

When treating a skeletal-muscular injury, physiotherapists will first .... the patient's injury. This means asking questions to find out things like what is injured, the type of injury and what .... they have. To help them find out what is wrong they might send the patient for a .... like an MRI scan. The physiotherapist will then come up with a set of .... to help aid recovery. They may also suggest other ...., for example, injections to reduce pain and swelling.

Q2 Carla plays **hockey** for her local team. During a match she **hurts her leg**. The **physiotherapist** says that she has injured a **muscle**, and treats it straight away.

a) The physiotherapist treats Carla's injury using the steps below. Write them out in the correct order.

compression	1. ....
elevation	2. ....
rest	3. ....
ice	4. ....

b) After the swelling on her leg has gone down, Carla's physiotherapist shows her a series of exercises to work through during the next few weeks. Number the boxes below to put the exercises in the correct order. Two have been done for you.

☐ **Gentle jogging to build up pre-injury levels of strength and muscle usage.**

☐ **Return to hockey training, gradually building up intensity.**

3 **Stretching and weight-bearing exercises to improve the strength of the injured muscle.**

☐ **Gentle exercise such as walking and swimming to regain movement and maintain aerobic fitness.**

1 **Simple stretching exercises to regain flexibility in the muscle.**

Top Tips: After a physiotherapist devises a programme for a patient or client, they don't just pat themselves on the back, put their feet up and leave them to get on with it. Instead they keep meeting up for a good gossip... err sorry, to check the person's progress and make sure the plan is working nicely.

Fitness Practitioners — Good Practice

Q1 A **careers adviser** has asked a class of GCSE students to write lists of their **personal qualities**. She will use these to help the students decide what kind of career they might be **suited** to. Three of the students' lists are shown below.

A
1) good listener
2) good communicator
3) good judgement
4) sensitive
5) works well in teams

B
1) hard-working
2) reliable
3) ambitious
4) competitive
5) blunt

C
1) imaginative
2) artistic
3) creative
4) thoughtful
5) original

a) Which student do you think is best suited to being a **fitness practitioner**? Circle the correct answer.

A **B** **C**

b) The careers adviser arranges for the students to meet Michael, a personal trainer.

i) Michael says it's important to develop a professional relationships with patients. Circle the words below that describe how a professional relationship should be.

emotional personal prejudiced detached indifferent dishonest

ii) Michael describes a difficult situation he once faced. A client had been given a special diet to help her lose weight. The client said she had stuck to the diet but wasn't losing weight.

Tick the boxes by the statements describing what a fitness practitioner **should** do in this situation.

- Tell the client off for not sticking to their diet. ☐
- Decide how to proceed based on what the client says and the evidence. ☐
- Talk to the client. Ask questions and listen carefully to her answers to try and understand why the diet is not working. ☐
- Offer the client money to stick to their diet. ☐
- Consider whether the diet needs changing so that it fits in better with the client's family or work life. ☐

iii) The students find Michael very easy to talk to. Give **three** reasons why it is important for fitness practitioners to have good communication skills.

1. ....

2. ....

3. ....

Mixed Questions — Unit 1: Topic 1

Q1 Lucy is worried that her **lifestyle** is putting her at risk of **coronary heart disease**. She joins a gym and is given a **personal trainer**.

a) Her personal trainer carries out a **baseline assessment** to assess Lucy's fitness. Suggest **two** things that Lucy's personal trainer may ask her about as part of her baseline assessment.

1. ....

2. ....

b) Being overweight is a risk factor for coronary heart disease. The personal trainer measures Lucy's height and weight so he can determine her body mass index. She is 1.58 m tall and weighs 83 kg.

i) Calculate Lucy's BMI.

$$\text{BMI} = \frac{\text{body mass in kg}}{(\text{height in m})^2}$$

....

....

ii) Fill in the table to the right with the correct ranges of BMI for **underweight**, **healthy weight**, **overweight** and **obese**.

BMI	Condition
<18.5	underweight
	healthy weight
	overweight
	obese

iii) Is Lucy overweight? Give a reason for your answer.

....

....

....

c) Lucy is concerned that since she has started exercising regularly, her urine is darker in colour and more concentrated.

i) Which of the following could explain the change in Lucy's urine? Tick **one** box.

- [ ] By doing exercise, she is losing more water from her body as sweat.
- [ ] She is drinking too much water.
- [ ] She is not sweating enough when exercising.

ii) Suggest **one** way in which Lucy could make her urine more pale and dilute.

....

d) Whilst exercising, Lucy tears a **ligament** in her ankle. Describe the role of a ligament in a joint.

....

....

Mixed Questions — Unit 1: Topic 1

Q2 Tom suffers from **asthma**. His doctor recommends that he does more **exercise**.

a) Asthma is caused by over-sensitive air passages in the breathing system.

i) What is the name of the pair of tubes that take air into the lungs?
Tick the correct box.

trachea ☐ bronchi ☐ diaphragm ☐

ii) **Gas exchange** in the human breathing system takes places in small sacs called **alveoli**.
Give **one** feature of alveoli that helps to speed up gas exchange.

....

b) Tom decides to join a local gym.

i) As part of his initial fitness assessment, Tom's trainer measures his **pulse rate**.
Describe how pulse rate is measured.

....

....

ii) While Tom is exercising he hurts a muscle in his leg.
Describe **four** steps the physiotherapist at the gym would use to treat Tom.

....

Think about the "RICE" method here.

....

Q3 Sanjay is taking a qualification to become a **personal trainer**.

a) As part of his qualification, Sanjay is learning about respiration and the heart.

i) Name the type of blood vessel that carries blood **away from** the heart.

....

ii) Tick the **two** boxes below that are next to **true** statements about respiration.

Anaerobic respiration is respiration without oxygen. ☐

Lactic acid is a waste product from aerobic respiration in humans. ☐

Carbon dioxide is a waste product from anaerobic respiration in humans. ☐

Glucose can be broken down in both aerobic and anaerobic respiration. ☐

b) Sanjay's tutor tells him that when he is dealing with clients and their fitness, Sanjay must think about '**the whole person**'. Explain what his tutor means by this.

....

....

Organisations Involved in Health Care

Q1 An elderly woman has fallen down some stairs. Her neighbour phones for an **ambulance** to take her to the **local hospital**.

a) Give **two** services the local hospital may provide to the public.

....

b) Suggest **one** place, other than a hospital, where she could go to be checked.

....

c) Why is it important that communities have **local** health care organisations, like hospitals?

....

Q2 A teacher at a local school has asked a **nurse** to come and talk to the pupils about the **National Health Service**.

a) Fill in the passage below using words from the list.

specialist care	hospitals	dentistry	some	gyms	all

The National Health Service (NHS) owns and runs the majority of the UK's .... It also provides many other health care services, such as .... The NHS makes sure that health care is available to .... citizens and that .... is provided, even if it's not available locally.

b) Apart from providing diagnoses and treatment, describe **one** other function of the NHS.

....

Q3 Aisha is a **manager** in the **NHS**. Most of her time is spent deciding how to **allocate resources** in the best possible way.

Which of the following are resources that Aisha will have to allocate? Circle the **three** correct answers.

money for buildings   patients   illnesses   equipment   staff

Top Tips: You never know when you might need health care — thankfully the good old NHS provides it for free. Make sure you know two examples of health care organisations for the exam.

People Involved in Health Care

Q1 Ryan is a **health care practitioner**. Dr Walker is a **general practitioner** (GP). Dr Walker asks Ryan to take a **blood sample** from a patient. He also asks Ryan to monitor the patient's **heart rate**.

a) Which of the following health care practitioners is Ryan?
Circle the correct answer.

nurse pharmacist dentist

b) i) Briefly describe what a **doctor** does.

....

....

ii) Describe **two** skills Dr Walker needs to do his job.

1. ....

....

2. ....

....

c) The patient may also have to see other health care practitioners.
Draw lines to match each health care practitioner to their **role**.

Nutritionist	Checks for problems with a patient's sight.
Pharmacist	Gives advice on the best foods to eat to stay healthy or reduce the symptoms of a disease.
Optician	Gives out medications to a patient that have been prescribed by a doctor.

Q2 Paul works for the Care Quality Commission. As part of his job he has to check that dentists are following **health and safety regulations** properly.

a) Suggest **one** example of something a dentist must do to make sure they're sticking to health and safety regulations.

....

b) Explain why health care practitioners have to follow regulations.

....

Public Health

Q1 Dr Spencer has a small doctor's surgery.

a) If one of his patients is having long-term treatment, Dr Spencer arranges **regular appointments** with them. Underline the reasons why this is a good idea.

It is good exercise for the patient to go to the doctor's surgery.

It can help strengthen the relationship between doctor and patient.

It allows the doctor to check whether the patient is improving.

It increases the income of the NHS.

It allows the doctor to keep up-to-date with the patient's medical history.

b) In Dr Spencer's waiting room there are several leaflets advising people on how to lead a healthier lifestyle.

i) How might people benefit from leading a healthier lifestyle? Tick **two** correct statements.

- ☐ People might have to take more medications.
- ☐ People might live longer.
- ☐ People might be less likely to get diseases.
- ☐ People might have more days off sick from work.

ii) In the waiting room there's also a poster which encourages people to get vaccinations. Why is it important that people get vaccinations?

....

....

Q2 Carrie has been diagnosed with **cancer** of the ovaries.

a) Carrie's doctor has told her that she can have an operation to have the cancer removed. He has told her the **operation success rate**. Explain why Carrie was given the operation success rate.

....

....

b) The doctor explained more than one method of treatment to Carrie. Did he need to do this?

☐ Yes ☐ No

Explain your answer.

....

Medical History

Q1 John goes to see his **doctor**. He says to her, "I've had a **bad cough** and a **sore head** for a few days. Also I feel very **tired** most of the time."

a) Tick the boxes to show whether the following statements are **true** or **false**.

	True	False
John has given the doctor information about how much exercise he does.	☐	☐
The doctor can use the information to help diagnose John's condition.	☐	☐
John has given the doctor information about his medication.	☐	☐
John has given the doctor information about his symptoms.	☐	☐

b) The doctor thinks John's lifestyle might be affecting the way he's feeling. List **three** questions the doctor might ask about John's lifestyle.

1. ....

2. ....

3. ....

Q2 Ann has recently moved to a new town and needs to **register** with a **doctor**. When she goes to the surgery she is given a form full of **questions** to answer.

a) One question asks if there is a history of cancer or diabetes in her family. Which of these statements correctly explains why her doctor would want this information? Tick any that apply.

☐ **So the doctor can register her family members as well.**

☐ **So the doctor knows whether Ann is more likely to get either disease.**

☐ **Ann won't be allowed to register with the new doctor if members of her family have had either disease.**

b) Why might the questionnaire ask if she is taking any long-term medication?

....

....

c) What other things might Ann be asked about? Underline the **two** correct answers.

how much TV she watches

if she's allergic to anything

whether she's had any previous illnesses

how often she has a bath

her annual income

Prioritising Treatment and Resources

Q1 A new **accident and emergency** department is due to open. Caroline's job will be to **manage its resources**.

a) Caroline has called a meeting with the accident and emergency staff to talk to them about her plans for managing resources. Underline **three** things that Caroline's likely to say at the meeting.

"We are going to practise dealing with major incidents."

"You are not allowed to have your mobile phone with you while you're working."

"We will be keeping a record of the type and amount of equipment we have."

"You are not allowed to lift a patient unless you have been properly trained."

"There's a staff rota so you can see when you need to be in work."

b) Accident and emergency departments only have a limited amount of money. Why is it important that an accident and emergency department manages its resources?

....

Q2 Henry is waiting in the **accident and emergency department** of a hospital with a suspected **broken arm**. He is frustrated because some people who arrived after him are being **treated before** him.

The table below shows the people needing treatment.

Name	Age	Condition
Henry	27	Suspected broken arm
Joe	5	Having an asthma attack, cannot breathe
Mary	83	Suspected broken arm
Philip	34	Major blood loss from deep cut on leg
Kate	26	Head injury, conscious but in a lot of pain

a) **i)** Who should be treated first? ....

ii) Give a reason for your answer.

....

b) Henry and Mary have similar injuries. Why is Mary treated before Henry?

....

c) What word is used to describe the process of prioritising patients' care? Circle the correct answer below.

treatment triage tourniquet

Treatment

Q1 Jenny takes her little girl, Rian, to see her GP. Rian has been finding it hard to **hear** the teachers at nursery. The GP **can't diagnose** Rian's problem.

a) What might the GP do next? Circle the correct answer below.

Tell Jenny to look on the internet to find out what's wrong with Rian.

Refer Rian to a general nurse for another opinion.

Refer Rian to a specialist service for tests on her ears.

b) Six weeks later Rian has been diagnosed as having an ear condition called glue-ear. Her GP can't prescribe any treatment that will help. Describe what the GP could do next to help Rian.

....

Q2 Mick has damaged one of the **discs** in his back. His doctor tells him about the **possible treatments**, which are described below.

Option 1: take painkillers to help the pain.

Option 2: take gentle exercise, e.g. walking or swimming.

Option 3: physiotherapy to ease pressure around the damaged disc.

Option 4: an operation to repair the damaged disc.

a) Mick is in a lot of pain, so his doctor prescribes the painkiller ibuprofen. Like many drugs, ibuprofen can cause side-effects.

Underline the reason why Mick's doctor has prescribed ibuprofen even though it could cause side-effects

WARNING:
may cause extreme hairstyles.

Side-effects only affect people who are already ill.

Without ibuprofen Mick's back will get worse.

The benefits outweigh the risks of side-effects.

b) Six weeks after Mick hurt his back it is still no better. His doctor recommends an operation to mend Mick's disc.

i) Suggest why Mick's doctor waited so long before advising an operation.

....

ii) When Mick goes to hospital for the operation he is asked to sign an 'informed consent' form. Why does he need to do this?

....

....

Pregnancy

Q1 A school nurse has produced a hand-out to give to pupils in a **sex education** class.

Fill in the gaps in the paragraph from the hand-out using words from the box.
You may use each word once or more than once.

cervix	fallopian tube	28	vagina	fertilised	uterus	ovaries

One of the two .... produces an egg every .... days. The egg passes into the .... where it may meet sperm that have entered through the .... during sexual intercourse. If the egg is .... by a sperm, it will attach itself to the lining of the .... and begin to develop into a baby. If the egg is not fertilised, it travels through the .... then out through the .... during a period.

Q2 An antenatal class is being shown the diagrams below. These show the uterus **before** pregnancy and how it will change **during** pregnancy.

Before pregnancy

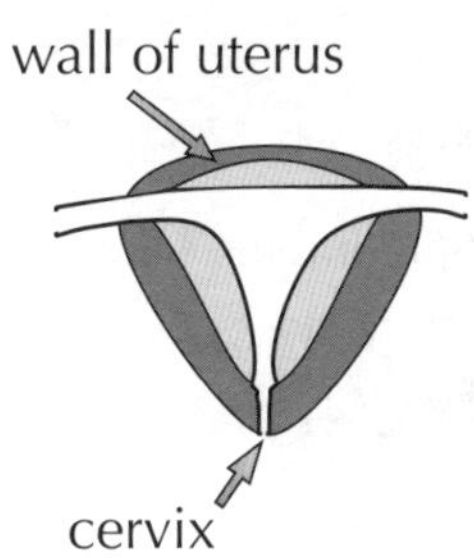

During pregnancy

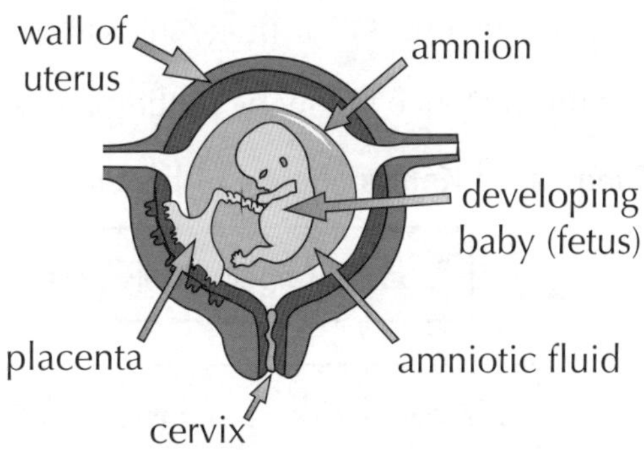

a) Describe what happens to the uterus during pregnancy.

....

b) What is the function of the following parts shown in the diagram?

i) amnion ....

ii) placenta ....

c) Describe what happens to each of the following parts during the birth of the baby.

i) amnion ....

ii) placenta ....

iii) uterus ....

iv) cervix ....

IVF

Q1 Josie and Johnny have been referred to a fertility clinic for IVF.
At the start of the treatment Josie is given **hormones**.

a) Why is Josie given hormones at the start of the treatment? Circle the correct answer below.

To stop her producing eggs. | To stop her from getting pregnant naturally. | To stimulate her egg production.

b) After the hormones have been given, the IVF treatment continues.
Number the following statements (1-4) to show the correct order of Josie and Johnny's IVF treatment.

- ☐ Josie's eggs are fertilised with Johnny's sperm in a lab and these are grown into embryos.
- ☐ Eggs are collected from Josie's ovaries.
- ☐ The embryos implant into the lining of the uterus.
- ☐ The embryos are transferred to Josie's uterus.

Q2 Katie has had IVF and is now pregnant with **triplets**.

a) Complete the sentence below by putting a tick in the correct box.

IVF increased Katie's chance of becoming pregnant with multiple babies because...

- ...lots of sperm were used to fertilise her eggs. ☐
- ...more than one embryo was transferred to her uterus. ☐
- ...the treatment caused her uterus to expand. ☐

b) When would Katie have found out she was carrying triplets?

....

c) Katie had counselling sessions before and during her IVF treatment.
Briefly describe **one** reason why Katie may have needed this counselling.

....

Top Tips: IVF is really useful for couples who want children but can't get pregnant naturally. Make sure you know all the stages involved, including monitoring the woman and counselling.

Antenatal Care

Q1 Misbah is pregnant. She goes to see her **midwife** for a routine antenatal appointment.

a) Briefly describe **one** thing midwives do when providing antenatal care.

....

....

b) Misbah has several checks at her antenatal appointment.
Circle **two** things that may be checked.

her weight | her hearing | her eyesight | her blood pressure

c) The midwife has arranged for Misbah to have an **ultrasound** scan.
The sentences below are about ultrasound scans.
Tick the boxes to show whether each sentence is **true** or **false**.

	True	False
i) Ultrasound scans are used to identify pre-eclampsia.	☐	☐
ii) Ultrasound scans are used to check the health of the baby.	☐	☐
iii) Ultrasound scans are used to check that the baby is growing normally.	☐	☐
iv) Ultrasound scans are used to check the weight of the mother.	☐	☐

Q2 Luanne is a midwife. She has just checked one of her patient's **urine samples** and is now worried that the patient may have **pre-eclampsia**.

a) What substance do you think was found in the urine sample?
Tick the correct answer below.

fat ☐ blood ☐ protein ☐ glucose ☐

b) What should Luanne do next to check if the patient has pre-eclampsia?
Underline the correct answer below.

Check the patient's weight.

Check the patient's blood pressure.

Take a blood sample from the patient.

c) Explain why pre-eclampsia is a worrying condition.

....

....

d) Name **one** other health problem that may be detected in pregnancy by testing a urine sample.

....

Blood Tests

Q1 Liam's skin has started to turn yellow. He needs a **blood test** to properly diagnose the problem, so Dr Chilton is taking a sample of Liam's blood.

a) Firstly, Dr Chilton puts a **tight band** around Liam's upper arm. Why does Dr Chilton do this? Circle the correct answer below.

To make the blood flow out of the veins below the band more quickly.

To hold Liam still.

To make the veins below the band fill with blood.

b) Next Dr Chilton looks closely at Liam's arm to find the best place to take blood from. Complete the following sentences by circling the correct word(s) in each pair.

Dr Chilton looks for a vein that is **far from** / **close to** the surface of the skin to take blood from. This is most likely to be found on the inside of the **elbow** / **wrist**.

c) Liam looks away when Dr Chilton takes blood from his arm. Put the steps below in the right order (1-3) to describe what's happening while Dr Chilton takes his blood.

☐ The syringe fills with blood.

☐ Dr Chilton inserts a needle attached to a syringe into Liam's arm.

☐ Dr Chilton pulls up the plunger of the syringe.

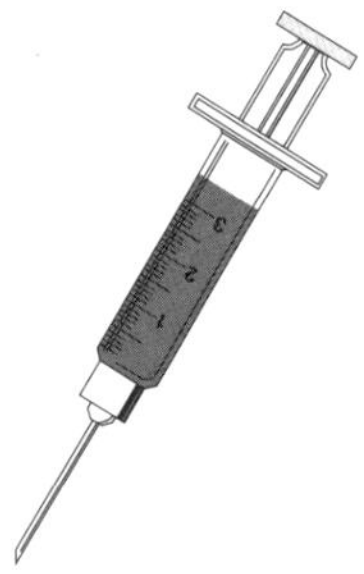

Q2 Jack has **spina bifida**. He's had the condition since he was born.

a) What is spina bifida?

....

b) i) Before he was born, doctors detected that Jack was at risk of spina bifida by looking at the results of a blood test. Which blood did they test? Tick the correct answer.

His mother's blood before she got pregnant. ☐

His mother's blood while she was pregnant. ☐

His mother's blood while Jack was being born. ☐

ii) What would the results of the blood test have shown? Circle the correct answer below.

high levels of glucose

high levels of alpha fetoprotein (AFP)

high levels of iron

Blood Tests

Q3 Janine is **pregnant** and is having a **blood test** done.

a) Tick the correct boxes below to show what the results of the blood test may show.

- ☐ Health problems with the mother.
- ☐ How many babies the mother is carrying.
- ☐ The date when the baby is due to be born.
- ☐ Birth defects.

b) A summary of the findings from Janine's blood test are shown below.

- High levels of inhibin A
- Low levels of unconjugated oestriol (uE3)
- Low levels of alpha fetoprotein (AFP)

These substances are all proteins or hormones.

Janine's doctor has written a report based on the findings of the blood test. Circle the correct words below to complete a sentence from the doctor's report.

The results of the blood test show that the **mother / baby** is at risk of having **anaemia / Down's syndrome**.

Q4 Jensen works in a **hospital**. Part of his job is to **order equipment** for the wards.

a) Jensen's in trouble at the moment because he forgot to order the **antiseptic wipes** used when taking a blood sample from a patient. What are antiseptic wipes needed for when taking a blood sample? Underline the correct answer below.

They sterilise the patient's skin after the blood's been taken.

They sterilise the patient's skin before the needle's inserted.

They sterilise the needle and syringe.

b) Jensen's also in trouble because he forgot to order the labels that go on blood sample tubes.

i) Give **one** piece of information that gets written on the labels.

....

ii) Explain why the labels that go on sample tubes are important.

....

....

Top Tips: Blood tests can identify lots of health problems. Make sure you're up to speed on the steps involved in giving a blood sample and what blood tests during pregnancy can show.

Post-Natal Care

Q1 Hamish is two weeks old. His mum is taking him for a **post-natal check**.

a) Where is this check most likely to be done? Circle the correct answer below.

at a local clinic | in an accident and emergency department | in a maternity ward

b) During his post-natal check, the health visitor checks Hamish's physical development.

i) Why are physical development tests done as part of post-natal care?
Tick the correct answer below.

☐ To check for behavioural problems with the baby.
☐ To pick up any problems with the baby's development as early as possible.
☐ To check whether the mother ate healthily while she was pregnant.

Hamish had his response to silly, long-armed men tested.

ii) Give **two** things that the health visitor might check about Hamish.

1. ....

2. ....

Q2 Mario is training to be a midwife. He is learning about a **score** that is given to a baby one minute and five minutes **after it's born**.

a) What is this score called?

....

b) Explain briefly why this score is given.

....

c) Mario is present at the births of three babies.
The table below shows the score each baby was given.

Baby	Score
Rapunzel	2
Raphael	7
Ronaldo	4

i) Pulse rate is one of the things that is measured to give each baby its score.
Give **two** other things that are measured to work out each baby's score.

1. .... 2. ....

ii) Based on the scores in the table, which baby would Mario be most worried about?

....

Post-Natal Care

Q3 The post-natal care of a baby includes monitoring its **growth**.

Complete the following passage using some of the words from the list.
You can only use each word once.

behaviour	regularly	foot	normally	occasionally	head	growth	length

After the birth, a baby's growth is .... monitored. This is done to make sure it's growing .... and to pick up on any .... problems. As well as weight, ... and .... size are also measured.

Q4 A **baby's mass** was recorded from birth to around the age of three.
The results are shown on the chart below.

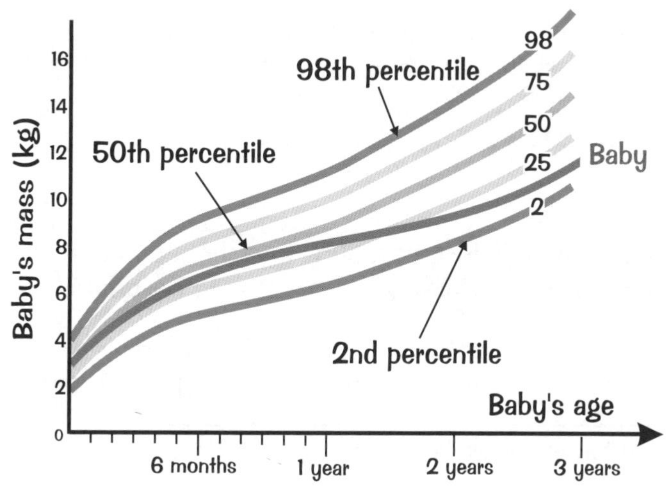

a) What name is given to charts like the one above? Circle the correct answer below.

development charts   growth charts   success charts

b) What is shown by the 50th percentile on this chart?
Circle the correct word in each pair to complete the sentence below.

The **mass** / **height** that **75%** / **50%** of babies will have reached at a certain age.

c) Doctors are usually concerned if a baby's mass is below the 2nd percentile. Based on this information and the chart above, would a doctor have been concerned about this baby? Explain your answer.

....

d) Which percentile was the baby's mass closest to when it was **one year** old?

....

Mixed Questions — Unit 1: Topic 2

Q1 Carol is starting **IVF** treatment. This means she needs to have a **blood test** to check her hormone levels.

a) i) Circle **three** things that the nurse needs in order to take a sample of Carol's blood.

pipette | tight band | sterile water | syringe | thermometer | sample tube

ii) Complete the sentence below by drawing a line to the correct box on the right.

When the nurse is taking a blood sample she needs to follow...

...health and safety regulations.

...her own regulations.

...a doctor's regulations.

...the leader.

b) Carol will soon be having some of her eggs collected from her ovaries. What happens next to the eggs in order to create embryos?

....

Q2 Rob was **rock scrambling** when he lost his footing and slipped into the lake below. His friend called the **emergency services**, who took Rob to **hospital**.

a) When Rob arrives at the hospital there are lots of people waiting to be treated. Number the boxes below to show the order in which these patients would be treated.

☐ A chef who has cut his finger while chopping vegetables.

☐ A child who is choking and cannot breathe.

☐ A lady who is bleeding from a head injury.

b) At the hospital, Rob is treated by several different medical practitioners. Give the title and role of **one** type of practitioner who may have treated Rob.

Title: .... Role: ....

....

c) Rob is told that he needs to have an X-ray on his leg. He needs to give his informed consent before the X-ray is taken, so he is told about the risks involved with having an X-ray. Give **two** other things he needs to be informed about in order to give informed consent.

1. ....

2. ....

Mixed Questions — Unit 1: Topic 2

Q3 Dr Grant is a GP that works for the **NHS**.

a) Describe **one** function of the National Health Service.

....

b) A new patient comes to see Dr Grant with backache.
Dr Grant asks the patient the following three questions about her general health.

1. Do you have any other symptoms?

2. Have you had any previous illnesses or injuries?

3. Are you allergic to anything?

Explain why Dr Grant has asked each of these questions.

....

....

....

Q4 Susie is **pregnant**. She has decided to employ a **private midwife** — this will ensure that she always sees the same person.

a) Give **one** advantage of regular contact between Susie and her midwife.

....

b) The midwife explains the changes that will happen to Susie's body during her pregnancy. Describe **two** changes the midwife would have explained.

1. ....

2. ....

c) **i)** At a routine appointment with her midwife, Susie has a sample of urine tested to see if she might have gestational diabetes. What substance is the urine tested for?

....

ii) Testing a urine sample is not enough to confirm a woman has gestational diabetes. What other test needs to be done?

....

Scientists and Environmental Protection

Q1 Paul works as an **environmental protection officer**.
His job is to collect and analyse evidence about the environment.

a) Give **two** scientific or technical skills that Paul might need to do his job.

1. ....

2. ....

b) Paul spends a lot of time in the laboratory. Suggest **one** health and safety regulation that Paul should be aware of while working in the laboratory.

....

....

If you're struggling to answer Q1 b), think about what you need to do to keep safe in the lab at school.

Q2 Read the passage below about the **Environment Agency** and answer the questions that follow.

The Environment Agency is a government-funded organisation set up in 1996 to protect the environment of England and Wales. One of its main roles is to protect people against flooding from rivers and the sea. This involves maintaining and improving flood defences, such as the Thames barrier — large gates on the river Thames that can be closed at high tide to protect London from flooding. The Environment Agency also issues flood warnings and advises people living near rivers what to do if there's a flood.

The Thames barrier.

a) Which of the following countries does the Environment Agency operate in?
Circle **two** correct answers.

England / Northern Ireland / Scotland / Wales

b) Where does the Environment Agency get its money from?

....

c) What is the **Thames barrier** designed to do?

....

d) Apart from maintaining the Thames barrier and other defences, give **two** things the Environment Agency does to help protect people from floods.

1. ....

2. ....

Top Tips: In the exam, make sure you read any information you're given carefully. If you just quickly skim over it, you might miss something important that will help you to answer the questions.

Good Laboratory Practice

Q1 Janet works for the Drinking Water Inspectorate monitoring **drinking water quality**. She has to follow good laboratory practice everyday to get reliable results.

a) Complete the following passage about good laboratory practice using the words given below.

same | contaminated | maintained | reduce | safety | training | practices

Good laboratory practice involves using common .... and procedures, so that different scientists will all carry out the tests in the .... way. Good laboratory practice helps to .... the chances of .... samples and unreliable results. All equipment should be well .... to ensure reliable results are produced. Staff should undergo continuous .... so they know about the best standard methods available. Following health and .... regulations is also important for good laboratory practice.

b) Circle the correct word(s) to complete the sentence about reliable results.

A set of results could be considered more reliable if the experiment had been reproduced by **different** / **the same** people and the **methods** / **results** are **the same** / **different**.

c) Janet works in an **accredited** laboratory. Circle the sentences about accreditation that are true.

Staff in an accredited lab are unable to work to a good level.

Accreditation shows that a lab cannot produce reliable results.

Accreditation shows that a lab is able to produce accurate and precise results.

Accreditation gives clients confidence in the lab's results.

d) Janet's laboratory has been sent a water sample as part of a **proficiency test**.

i) What are proficiency tests used for?

....

....

ii) The graph shows the proficiency test results from five different labs. Janet works for lab B. Has her lab passed the proficiency test? Give a reason for your answer.

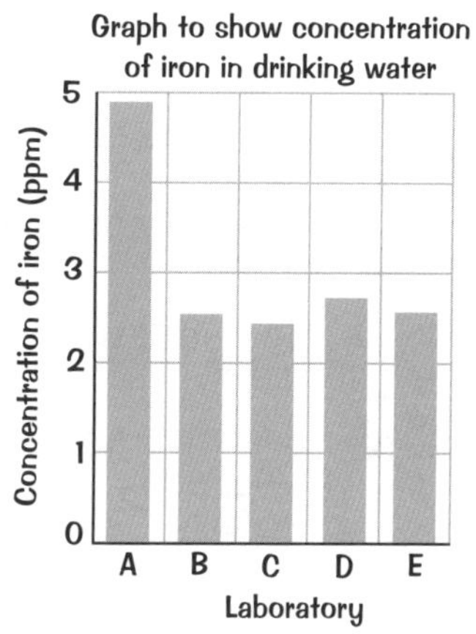

....

....

Taking Samples

Q1 Abdul is an **environmental protection officer**.
He is **collecting samples** of river water to check for pollution.

Complete the following passage using the words below. You should only use each word once.

sealed representative tampering labels deteriorating

When collecting samples from the river, Abdul should make sure he collects lots of samples from different places. This will make sure his samples are ....
Any samples collected should be stored in .... bags or containers to avoid contamination. The containers should also have .... stating what the samples are of and where and when they were taken.
Abdul can help prevent the evidence from .... by storing it properly. The samples might also need to be kept locked away to prevent anyone from .... with them.

Q2 Some scientists sample **living organisms** to help them **monitor** the **environment**.

a) Write the letter 'T' or 'F' in the box to show whether the statement below is true (T) or false (F). ☐

Scientists sample the organisms living in the oceans to monitor the effect of climate change.

Mayfly nymphs and **sludge worms** are often used to show whether an area is polluted or not.

b) What is the name for an organism used in this way?

....

Juanita recorded the number of each species in water samples taken at three different distances away from a sewage outlet. Her results are shown on the right.

Distance (km)	No. of mayfly nymphs	No. of sludge worms
1	3	20
2	11	14
3	23	7

c) What can you say about the two organisms from these results? Circle the correct word to complete the following sentences.

i) Mayfly nymphs prefer water that **does** / **doesn't** contain sewage.

ii) Sludge worms prefer water that **does** / **doesn't** contain sewage.

d) Bacteria found in water can use up lots of oxygen. Sewage causes bacterial populations in water to increase. Suggest why sewage may **decrease** the number of mayfly nymphs.

....

....

Visual Examination

Q1 Chantelle works for the **Environment Agency**.
She specialises in dealing with the aftermath of **floods**.

a) When Chantelle arrives at the scene of a flood she starts by visually examining the area.
Give **four** ways that Chantelle can record what she sees.

1. ....

2. ....

3. ....

4. ....

A helicopter takes aerial photographs of the area. Chantelle uses these photos and a grid map of the lake to make a diagram of the flood area. Her diagram is shown below.

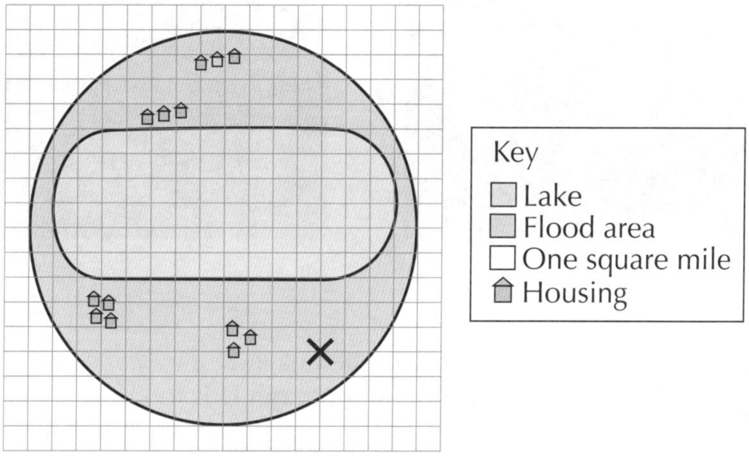

b) Chantelle takes measurements of the depth of the water at the point marked X on the diagram.
If Chantelle took lots of measurements at point X, she wouldn't always get the same result.
Explain why.

....

....

c) Chantelle needs to calculate the area affected when a lake floods.

i) Use the diagram to estimate the area covered by the lake.

.... square miles

ii) Calculate the area of the flood, including the lake.
Use the equation, area of a circle = $\pi \times r^2$,
where $\pi = 3.14$ and r = radius of the circle.

The radius is the distance from the centre of the circle to the edge.

....

.... square miles

iii) Use your answers from parts **i)** and **ii)** to calculate the area of the flood **not** including the lake.

.... square miles

Visual Examination

Q2 Chris is an **environmental protection officer** inspecting a local industrial site. He takes photographs of some **chemical storage barrels**. The photographs he took are shown below.

a) Chris is unhappy with the quality of some of the images.
For example, he thinks that the **contrast** in **photograph D** is too low.

i) What is meant by the term contrast?

....

....

ii) Chris also thinks that the **focus** isn't sharp enough in one of the images.
Which of the photographs, **A**, **B**, or **C**, is Chris referring to?

....

b) Which of the photographs, **A**, **B** or **C**, has the highest **magnification**?

....

c) Chris wants to know approximately how big the barrels are.
Use the scale to estimate the **length** (in **m**) of the barrel marked on **photograph C**.

....

Top Tips: For the exam, make sure you know how to calculate the **area** of shapes like rectangles and circles — and also make sure you've practised using a **linear scale**, such as a ruler.

Types of Testing

Q1 Alisha is using **litmus paper** to test the **acidity** of some **soil**.

a) Circle the correct word in each pair to complete the sentences about litmus paper.

i) Blue litmus paper turns red in **alkalis / acids**.

ii) Red litmus paper turns blue in **alkalis / acids**.

b) What kind of test is the litmus test? Circle the correct answer.

Qualitative   Semi-quantitative   Quantitative

Q2 James is investigating claims that **chemical waste** from a factory is ending up in local streams. He knows the chemical is **alkaline** and the water usually has a slightly **acidic pH**.

a) **i)** Name a solution, other than litmus, that James could use to test the pH of the water.

....

ii) What kind of results are produced by the test you named in **i)**? Circle the correct answer.

Qualitative   Semi-quantitative   Quantitative

iii) What **colour** should the solution you named in **i)** become when added to the chemical waste? Tick the correct box.

☐ Yellow

☐ Purple

☐ Red

b) James adds a few drops of a pH testing solution to samples taken from four streams near to the factory. The pH scale for the solution used is shown below.

i) Use the words given below to complete the pH scale diagram.

Neutral   Alkalis   Acids

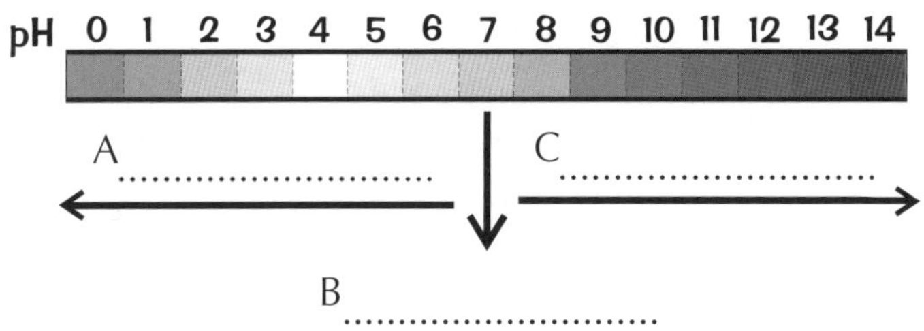

ii) The results of James's tests are shown on the right. Which of the samples could contain the chemical waste?

....

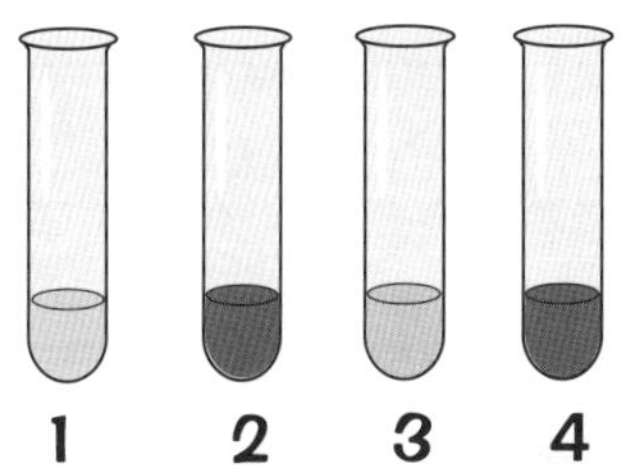

Types of Testing

Q3 Shabnam wants to find out roughly how much **nitrogen** is present in two **soil samples**. She has two different types of **test kit** she could use to do the job.

a) The test kits are described below.

Draw lines to match the description of each kit to the type of test it is.

Kit 1 — tells you roughly how much nitrogen is present in the soil using a colour matching chart.

Kit 2 — gives you an accurate number for the level of nitrogen in the soil.

Quantitative

Qualitative

Semi-quantitative

b) Shabnam decides to use Kit 1. She follows the instructions in the kit and observes the colour change for each soil sample. Her test results are shown below on the left and the key to the results is shown below on the right.

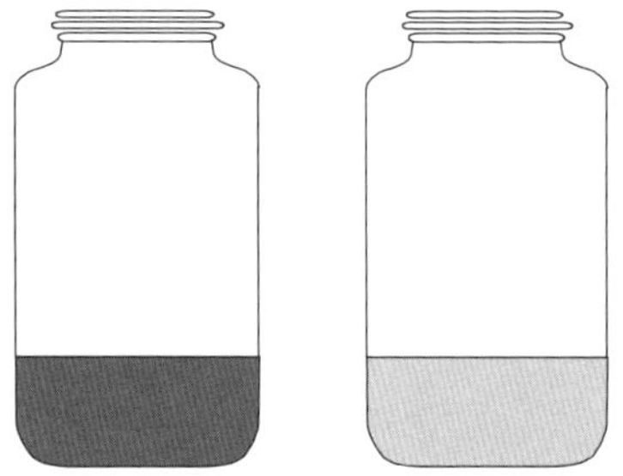

Soil sample 1 Soil sample 2

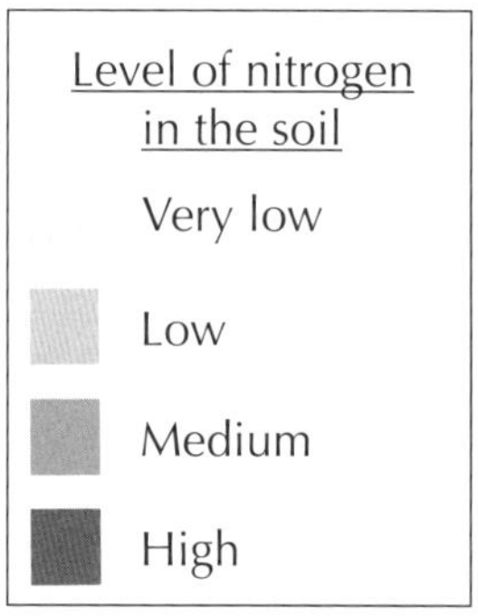

Key to results

What do the results of the tests indicate about the nitrogen level in each of the soil samples?

Soil sample 1 ....

Soil sample 2 ....

c) Dean is Shabnam's colleague. He thinks he has another way of determining the amount of nitrogen in soil. He says,

"If the plants growing in the soil have green leaves, there's probably **enough** nitrogen present. If the plants growing in the soil have yellow leaves, there's probably **not enough** nitrogen present."

Is Dean's method **qualitative**, **quantitative** or **semi-quantitative**? Explain your answer.

....

....

Top Tips: You really do need to know the difference between qualitative, quantitative, and semi-quantitative tests — so make sure you can answer all the questions on this page and the previous one. In the exam, if you get given some results from a test you've not come across before, don't panic. You'll be given all the information you need to answer the question.

Testing Water Quality

Q1 Circle the correct word in each pair to complete the sentences below.

Some solids dissolve when you mix them with water. You can tell the solids have dissolved when you can't **smell / see** them any more. The water and dissolved solids form a **solution / suspension** — if you filter this, you **will / won't** be able to separate the solids from the water. Some solids mix with water, but they don't dissolve in it — these are called **suspended / concentrated** solids. These solids make the water look **cloudy / clear** and they **can / can't** be separated from the water using filter paper.

Q2 Sophie is measuring the **turbidity** of the water in a local pond.

a) **i)** What is meant by the term 'turbidity'? Tick the box next to the correct answer below.

- ☐ **How wet a liquid is.**
- ☐ **How warm a liquid is.**
- ☐ **How cloudy a liquid is.**
- ☐ **How acidic a liquid is.**

ii) Is water with lots of **suspended solids** in it likely to have a high or low turbidity? Underline the correct answer below.

high turbidity / low turbidity

b) Sophie is using a **turbidity meter** to measure the turbidity of the pond water. A turbidity meter measures the amount of **light** that travels through a liquid. According to the meter, only a small amount of light can travel through the pond water. Does this mean the pond water has a high or low turbidity? Explain your answer.

....

....

c) A **turbidity tube** can also be used to measure turbidity.

i) What is a turbidity tube?

....

ii) Describe how Sophie could use a turbidity tube to measure the turbidity of the water.

....

....

....

....

Mixed Questions — Unit 1: Topic 3

Q1 Michelle is an **environmental protection officer**. She is carrying out a survey of the wildlife in an area of protected woodland.

a) Michelle makes a sketch of a butterfly she finds. She's not sure what species it is, so she compares her sketch to a sketch in a reference book. The two sketches are shown below.

Michelle's sketch

Reference book sketch

i) Suggest **two** features of the butterflies that Michelle might compare.

1. ....

2. ....

ii) Is the butterfly Michelle found the same as the one in the reference book? Give a reason for your answer.

....

....

b) Tick the boxes below to show whether the following statements about Michelle's job are **true** or **false**.

	true	false
i) Michelle needs a good understanding of laws relating to the environment to do her job.	☐	☐
ii) Michelle works outside, so she doesn't need to worry about health and safety regulations.	☐	☐
iii) Having keen observation skills will help Michelle to collect her data.	☐	☐
iv) Michelle needs very few scientific skills to do her job.	☐	☐

c) Michelle also collects information on **indicator organisms** living in a **stream** that runs through the woodland. Explain how indicator organisms can help Michelle to determine the level of **pollution** in the stream.

....

....

....

Mixed Questions — Unit 1: Topic 3

Q2 The **Environment Agency** has sent out a scientist to investigate a ship that is spilling **toxic chemicals** into the sea.

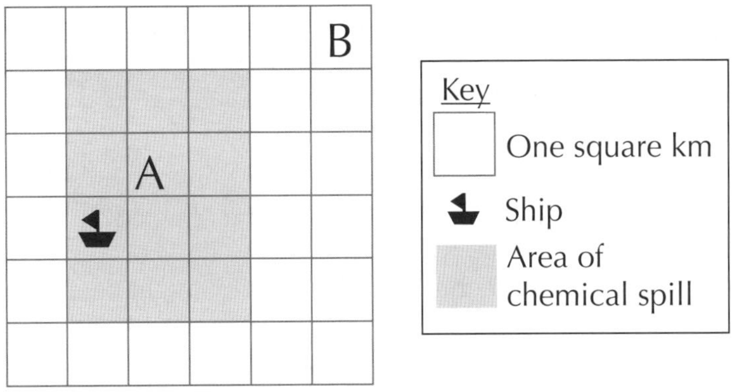

a) The diagram above shows the area of the chemical spill.
Calculate the area of the chemical spill.

.... square km

b) A scientist collects a sample of sea water from area A and area B and stores them in separate, sealed containers. Suggest **one** reason why the samples were stored like this.

....

c) The scientist tests whether the samples are acidic or alkaline using **litmus paper**.

- **Blue litmus paper turns red in the sample from area A.**
- **Red litmus paper turns blue in the sample from area B.**

What do these results tell you about each of the samples?

....

....

d) Apart from collecting data on water pollution, give **three** things that the Environment Agency does.

1. ....
2. ....
3. ....

Top Tips: You need to know what the colour changes involved in a litmus test mean. Luckily, there are only two colours involved — so it shouldn't be too difficult to learn them.

Scientists Protecting the Public

Q1 Alex is a **scene of crime officer**. She works for the police.

a) What does a scene of crime officer do?
Tick **one** box.

Records details of crime scenes and collects any useful evidence. ☐

Analyses evidence found at crime scenes in the laboratory. ☐

Arrests criminals found at crime scenes. ☐

Cleans up crime scenes once all the evidence has been collected. ☐

b) Give **one** example of a scientific or technical skill that Alex might need to do her job.

....

c) Many police forces send evidence collected from crime scenes off to private companies that provide **forensic science services**.

Give **two** examples of forensic science services that might be provided by these companies.

1. ....

2. ....

Q2 Theo works as a **public analyst** for the **Food Standards Agency**.

a) What tasks might Theo carry out as part of his job? Circle **two** correct answers below.

Monitoring air quality.

Providing advice on food-borne diseases.

Reviewing restaurants for the local paper.

Making sure products are labelled correctly.

Working with businesses to reduce pollution.

b) Public analysts often play an important role in their **local community**.

Other than those you circled in part **a)**, give **one** example of a task that Theo might carry out at work to benefit his local community.

....

c) Give **one** example of a **scientific skill** that Theo will need in order to do his job.

....

d) What **legislation** might Theo need to have a good understanding of in order to do his job?

....

Colorimetry

Q1 **Colorimetry** can be used to calculate the concentration of chemicals.

a) What does a colorimeter measure?

....

b) What type of result does colorimetry produce? Tick the correct answer.

- Qualitative ☐
- Semi-quantitative ☐
- Quantitative ☐

c) Colorimetry involves comparing a solution of unknown concentration to **standard reference solutions**. What is a standard reference solution?

....

Q2 Christopher is measuring the amount of carbohydrate in a drink to make sure the product is **labelled correctly**. He uses a chemical that turns blue when carbohydrate is present. The **more** carbohydrate, the deeper the shade of **blue**. Christopher uses **colorimetry** to measure the colour.

Christopher measures the absorbance of some reference samples of known carbohydrate concentration. His results are given below.

Carbohydrate concentration (g/ml)	Absorbance (absorbance units)
0.2	0.25
0.4	0.40
0.6	0.60
0.8	0.75
1.0	1.0

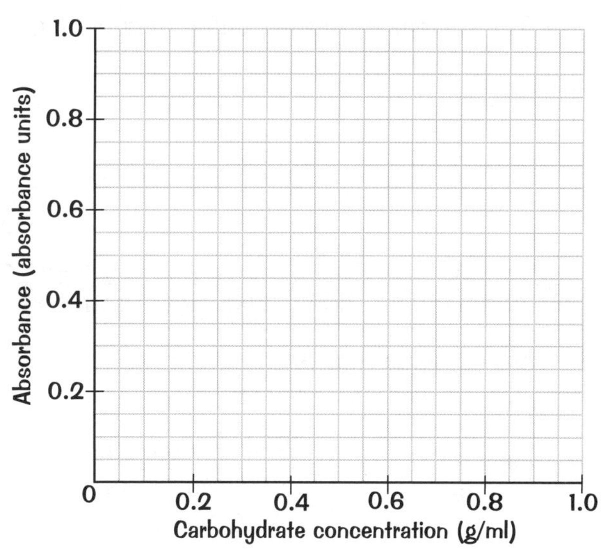

a) Use Christopher's results to draw a calibration graph, with a line of best fit, on the axes above.

b) The absorbance of an unknown drink sample is **0.55** absorbance units. Use the graph to work out the concentration of carbohydrate in the unknown sample. Show your working on the graph.

....

Top Tips: If you have to draw a line of best fit in the exam, don't just join up the dots. Use a **ruler** and try to draw a single line through, or as near to, as many of the data points as possible.

Chromatography

Q1 **Chromatography** is a method used for separating chemical mixtures.

a) Number the following statements (1-5) to show the correct method for carrying out **paper chromatography**.

- ☐ Compare the results to reference materials.
- ☐ Draw a line across the bottom of a piece of filter paper.
- ☐ Allow time for the solvent to seep up the paper.
- ☐ Place spots of the samples to be tested at regular intervals along the line.
- ☐ Hang the sheet in a beaker of solvent.

b) Complete the following passage using some of the words from the list below, to describe how paper chromatography works.

different similar dissolve stationary mobile

In paper chromatography, substances are separated by the movement of a solvent (known as the .... phase) through a medium (known as the .... phase). The solvent rises up the filter paper and when it reaches the spots of sample, the chemicals in the sample ....
The solvent carries the different chemicals in the sample up the filter paper at .... rates.

Q2 An **unknown mixture** was analysed using **paper chromatography**.
The chromatogram shown below was produced.

a) The chromatogram has been **developed**. Why might this have been done?
Circle the correct answer below.

To show up colourless spots. To stop the spots from moving further up the chromatogram. To stop the spots from fading.

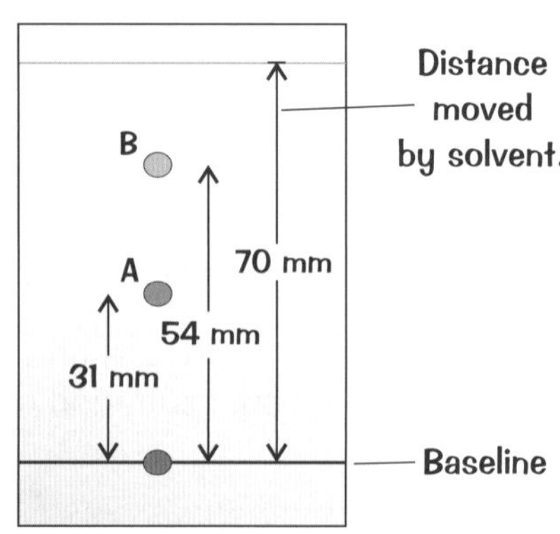

b) The chromatogram shows two substances were present in the mixture — substance **A** and substance **B**.
Use the formula to work out the R_f value of each substance.

$$R_f = \frac{\text{distance travelled by substance}}{\text{distance travelled by solvent}}$$

i) Substance A ....

ii) Substance B ....

Chromatography

Q3 Ella is using **paper chromatography** to compare the **ink** used on a **threatening letter** with the ink found in three **suspects' printers**.

a) Circle the correct word in each pair to complete the sentence below.

The **solvent** / **gas** used in paper chromatography depends on the **solvent** / **sample** being tested. Some compounds dissolve well in water but others are more soluble in **non-aqueous** / **aqueous** solvents.

b) When Ella analyses the ink from the threatening letter and the ink from the suspects' printers she obtains the chromatogram shown on the right.

Suggest which ink could have been used to produce the letter.

....

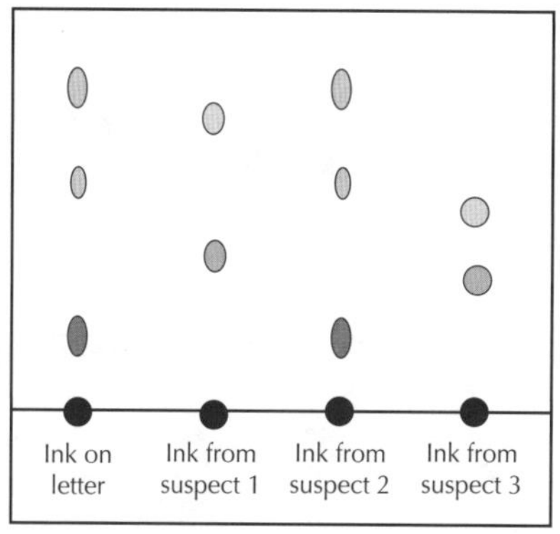

Q4 A scientist at the **Food Standards Agency** is testing some foods for banned **food colourings** using paper chromatography. She compares the results from three fruit juices with **reference samples** for two banned food colourings.

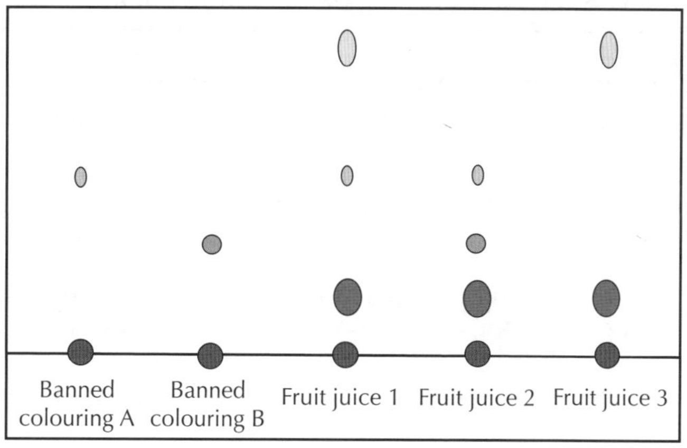

Tick the boxes below to show which colouring, if any, each of the fruit juices contains.

Compare the spots contained in the colourings and the juices.

	contains colouring A	**contains colouring B**	**contains neither**
Fruit juice 1	☐	☐	☐
Fruit juice 2	☐	☐	☐
Fruit juice 3	☐	☐	☐

Microscopes

Q1 Mohammad works for the local council as a **public analyst**. He inspects food service companies and monitors their **food hygiene practices**. He often takes samples from the food preparation areas to inspect under a **light microscope**.

a) Label these two parts of a light microscope.

i) ....

....

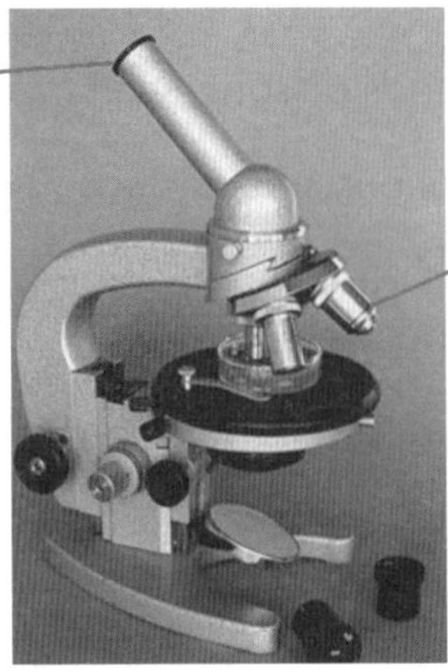

ii) ....

....

b) Draw lines to match the parts labelled above to their purpose.

i — magnifies the image

ii — allows the scientist to view and magnify the image

c) Circle the correct word in each pair to complete the paragraph below.

> Microscopes use **mirrors** / **lenses** to magnify images.
>
> This makes images look **smaller** / **bigger** and allows **more** / **less** detail to be seen.

d) Calculate the magnifying power of Mohammad's microscope.
His eyepiece lens has a magnification of **×10** and his objective lens has a magnification of **×40**.

....

Q2 Forensic scientists are comparing **pollen samples** taken from a crime scene to pollen found on a suspect's clothes. To do so, they are using a **scanning electron microscope**.

a) Suggest why they are using a scanning electron microscope rather than a light microscope.

....

b) Are scanning electron microscopes more or less **expensive** than light microscopes?

....

c) The scientists **can't** use their scanning electron microscope to view **living samples**. Explain why.

....

....

Interpreting Images from Microscopes

Q1 Residents of a town have complained of stomach upsets, possibly caused by contaminated **drinking water**. The water company that supplies the town takes water from a reservoir, **treats** it and stores it in tanks. A scientist collects water **samples** from the reservoir (**A**) and tanks (**B**) to check for **bacteria** that may cause illness.

The picture shows the stained (coloured) samples under a light microscope. The bacteria have been labelled and a key has been included to help with your descriptions.

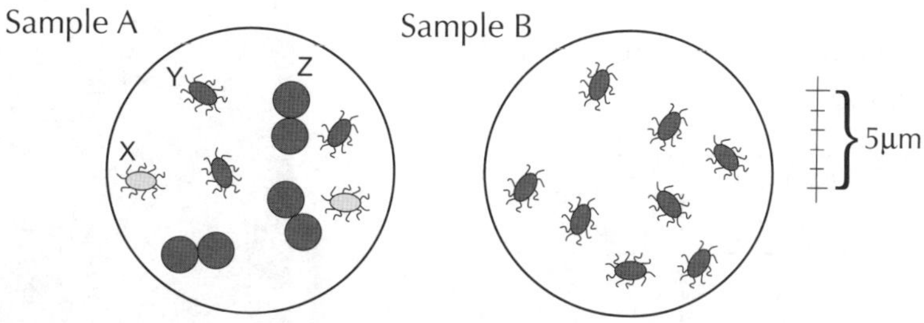

Reference Sample

- Red staining diplococci
- Red staining bacilli with flagella
- Violet staining diplococci
- Violet staining bacilli with flagella

a) Use the reference samples to identify the three types of bacteria.

X ....

Y ....

Z ....

b) Complete the table below by counting and measuring the main features in each sample.

Bacteria	Number in Sample A	Number in Sample B	Width (µm)
X	2		
Y			
Z			

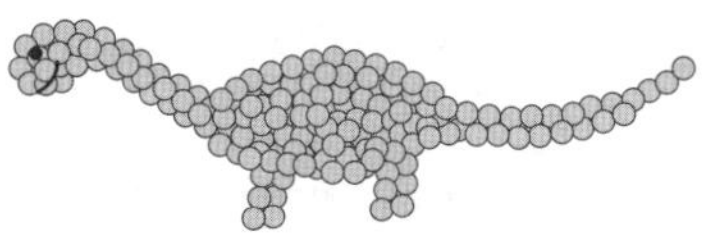

Josie was shocked to see a Diplodocus under the microscope

c) One type of red staining diplococci is known to commonly cause stomach upsets. Is it likely that the residents' stomach upsets have been caused by this red staining diplococci? Give a reason for your answer.

....

....

Interpreting Images from Microscopes

Q2 The police have found a dead body in a park. The autopsy found that the man has **water** in his lungs, which indicates he **drowned**. The pathologist collects a sample of the water for analysis. Forensic scientists can estimate where a person drowned by looking at the number and type of different **diatoms** (types of algae) in the water. The diatom composition is unique.

The electron micrograph of the diatoms found in a small volume of the water sample is shown on the right.

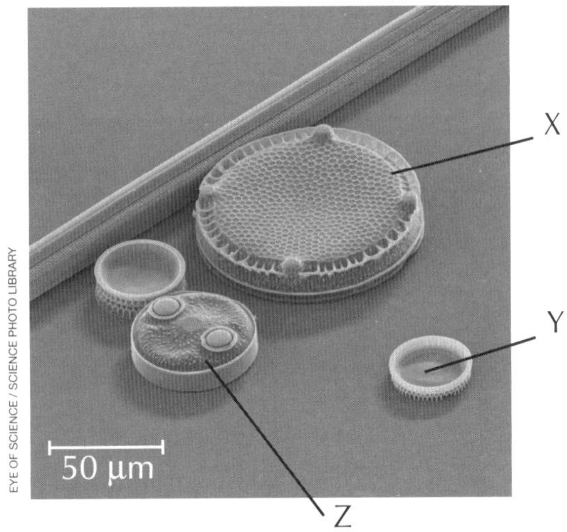

a) Complete the table about the main features of the electron micrograph.

Diatom	Number in sample	Diameter (µm)
X		
Y		
Z		

Here are some reference diagrams of diatoms.

***Eupodiscus* species**

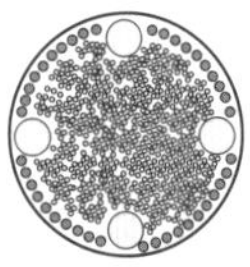

***Paralia* species**

***Campylosira* species**

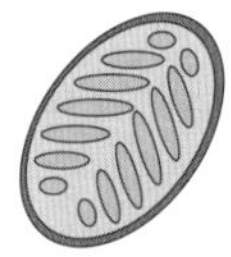

***Auliscus* species**

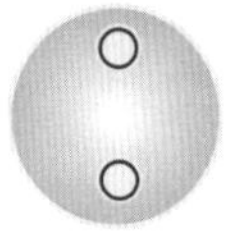

***Arachnoidiscus* species**

***Cyclotella* species**

b) Use the reference diagrams to identify the diatoms found in the water sample from the man's lungs.

X ....

Y ....

Z ....

The forensic scientist collects water samples from three different rivers in the area. The table on the right shows the diatoms found in each sample.

River	Diatoms present
1	*Auliscus* species *Arachnoidiscus* species *Paralia* species
2	*Paralia* species *Auliscus* species *Eupodiscus* species
3	*Camplylosira* species *Cyclotella* species *Arachnoidiscus* species

c) Which river might the man have drowned in?

....

Top Tips: Remember — interpreting electron micrographs is the same as interpreting images from light microscopes — **describe**, **count**, **measure** and **identify** the main features. Easy.

More on Visual Examination

Q1 A **stolen credit card** has been recovered by the police.
It was sent to the **forensics laboratory** for **fingerprint dusting**.

a) The fingerprint shown on the right is obtained from the credit card:

Fingerprint from credit card

There are **three** main types of fingerprint pattern.
Name the types of pattern shown below.

A ....

B ....

C ....

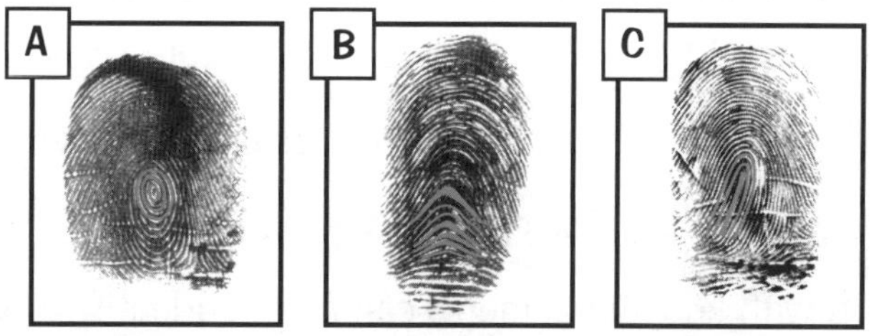

b) What is the main type of **pattern** on the fingerprint found on the credit card? ....

Q2 A **forensic scientist** is analysing a hair sample found at the scene of a crime.
The picture below shows the hair sample found at the **crime scene** under a light microscope.

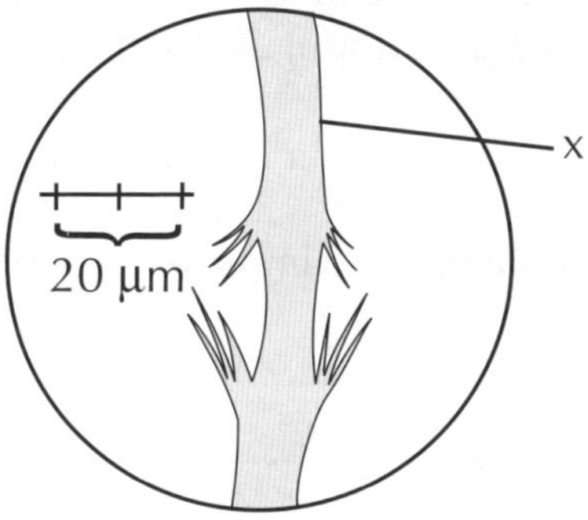

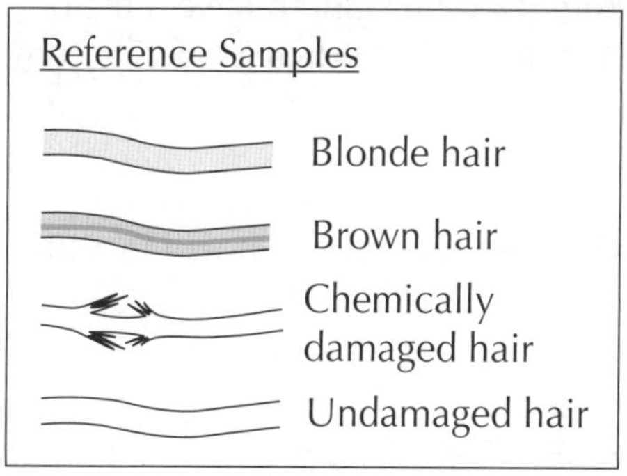

a) What is the diameter of the hair at point X?

....

Use the scale on the pictures to measure the diameter.

b) Other than diameter, give **two** features of the hair.

....

....

c) The hair sample to the right belongs to a **suspect**. Does the sample taken from the suspect match that found at the crime scene?
Give a reason for your answer.

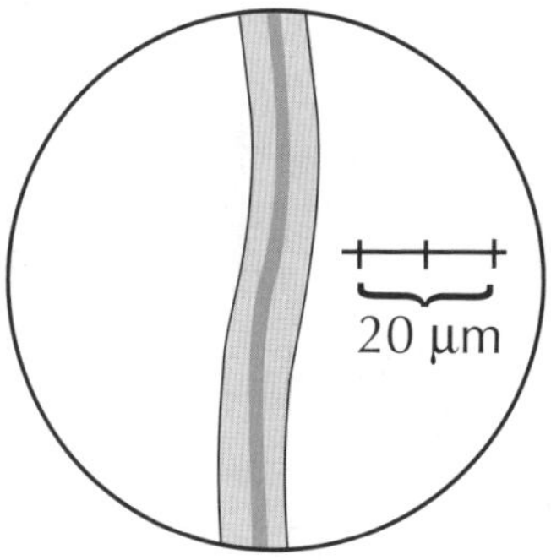

....

....

....

Electrophoresis

Q1 **DNA profiling** is an important tool, widely used by forensic scientists to link a suspect to a crime scene.

a) Complete the passage about DNA profiling using words from the list below.

unique	identical twins	electrophoresis	DNA	small

DNA profiling uses .... to compare

.... fragments. It's useful because everyone's DNA is

.... (except ....).

Comparisons with known fragments can help to identify unknown fragments.

DNA can be extracted from .... biological samples.

b) Give **two** samples that scientists might collect that contain DNA.

1. .... 2. ....

c) Some people want to have a national DNA database of everyone in the country, but others disagree. Give **one** reason why some people might be against storing DNA in a national database.

....

d) Give **one** example of how DNA profiling technology has helped to **improve** law enforcement.

....

....

Q2 The **Food Standards Agency** is investigating the claim that a caviar manufacturer is selling cheap (salmon or whitefish) caviar as expensive (beluga) caviar. They compare the **DNA profile** from two random samples of caviar taken from the manufacturer to reference DNA profiles from salmon, beluga and whitefish caviar.

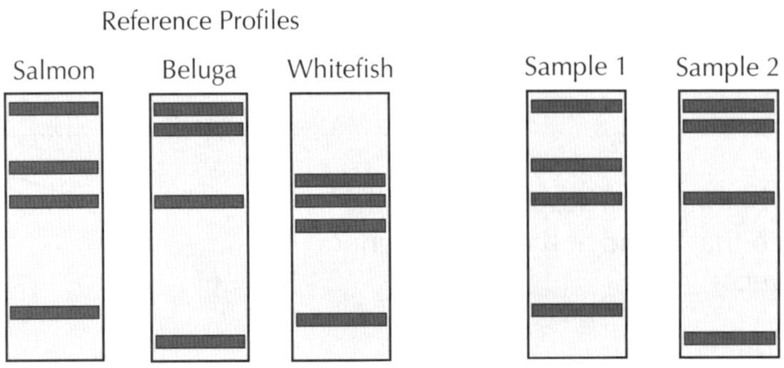

Compare the bands from the reference samples with those from the caviar samples.

What conclusions can be drawn from these results?

....

....

Mixed Questions — Unit 1: Topic 4

Q1 Police are investigating the **shooting** of a young man. A **bullet** collected from the crime scene and a **blood sample** collected from the jumper of a suspect have been sent away for **forensic analysis**.

The bullet used in the shooting is examined using a light microscope.

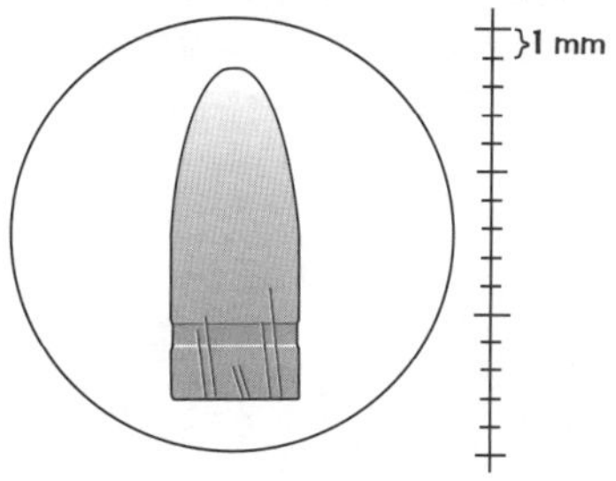

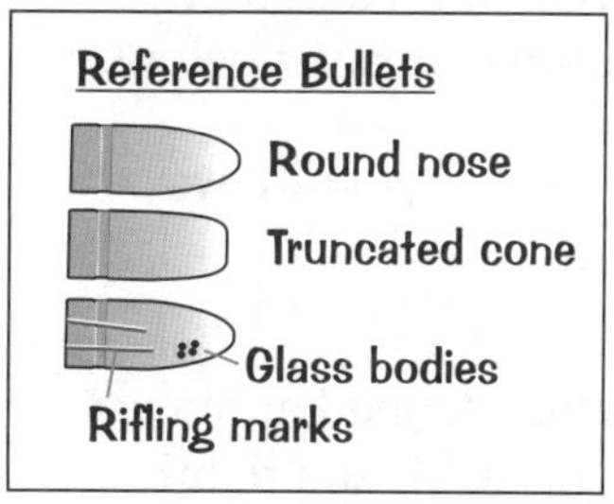

a) Describe the main features of the bullet using the reference bullets to help.

....

b) Measure the width of the bullet at it's widest point.

....

c) The picture on the right shows a bullet fired from the gun of a suspect.

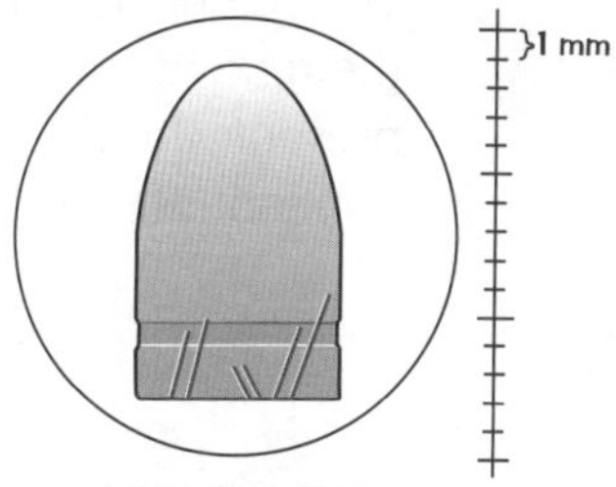

i) List one **similarity** between the bullet from the suspect's gun and the bullet retrieved from the crime scene.

....

ii) Do you think the suspect's gun was used in the shooting? Give a reason for your answer.

....

....

d) The microscope used to examine the bullets has an objective lens magnification of **×10** and an eyepiece lens magnification of **×4**. Work out the magnifying power of the microscope.

....

e) The scientists use **DNA profiling** to compare the DNA from the blood found on the suspect's clothing with the DNA of the victim. The results are shown below.

i) Name the technique used to produce the DNA profiles.

....

ii) What conclusion can you draw from the DNA profiles?

....

....

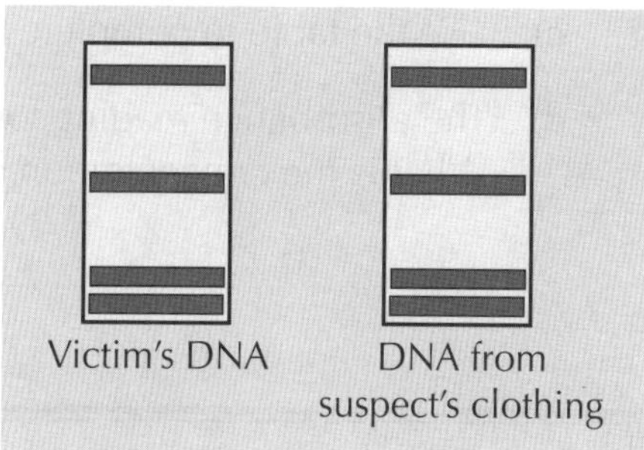

Mixed Questions — Unit 1: Topic 4

Q2 A scientist working for the **Food Standards Agency** uses **paper chromatography** to test for banned additives in a fizzy drink. She compares the results from the fizzy drink with reference samples for **three banned additives**. The chromatogram she produces is shown below.

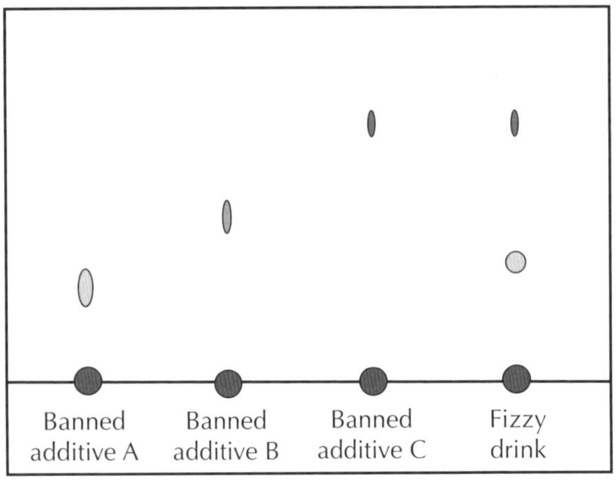

a) What type of result does chromatography produce? Circle the correct answer below.

Qualitative **Semi-quantitative**

Quantitative

b) The scientist believes that banned additive **C** is present in the fizzy drink. Is she right? Explain your answer.

....

....

....

The scientist then uses **colorimetry** to determine the exact **concentration** of the banned additive in the fizzy drink. She adds a chemical that will turn red if the additive is present. The more additive present, the deeper the shade of red. The absorbance readings from reference samples of known concentrations are given in the table below.

Concentration (parts per million)	Absorbance (absorbance units)
10	0.60
20	0.75
30	0.80
40	0.90
50	1.0

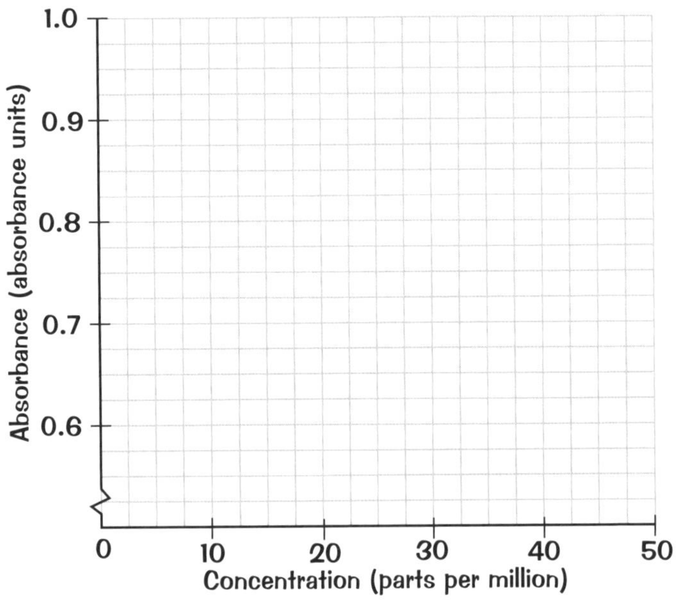

c) Use the table to complete the calibration graph, including a line of best fit.

d) The absorbance reading for her sample of fizzy drink is **0.85**.
What is the concentration of the banned additive?

....

Top Tips: At last, the end of another workbook section. Make sure you can answer these Mixed Questions. Just like the exam questions, they test you on a variety of different material.

Designing Sports Equipment

Q1 Shazma is a **trading standards officer**. She has written a leaflet explaining why **product standards** are important.

a) Complete the following extract from Shazma's leaflet using words from the list below.

injury **tested** **quality** **fire** **safe**

When people buy products they want to be sure the products are ....
If a product conforms to a particular standard, it will have been ....
thoroughly, for example to make sure that it doesn't cause ....
and won't catch .... under normal use. Standards also ensure that the
products are consistently of a high ....

b) Shazma's leaflet contains some information about organisations that help to promote good product standards, for example the **British Standards Institution (BSI)**.

i) What does it mean if a product displays the **BSI Kitemark**?

....

....

ii) Name **one** other organisation that helps to ensure good product standards.

....

Q2 Lucy wants to become a **material scientist**. Her careers advisor tells her to make a list of the skills she'll need to do the job, but Lucy is having difficulty coming up with ideas.

Lucy's list is shown on the right. Complete the list by writing down **two** more skills that material scientists need to do their job.

1) Good knowledge of materials and their properties.

1. ....

2. ....

Q3 The **CGP Trampoline Company** is one of Cumbria's smallest trampoline manufacturers.

The company recommends that the **maximum weight limit** for one of their trampolines is **100 kg**. However, they build the trampolines to safely support loads of up to **500 kg**.

Suggest why the company builds their trampolines with this safety margin.

....

....

Mechanical Properties

Q1 Circle the correct word in each pair to show whether the following diagrams show objects under **compression** or **tension**.

a)

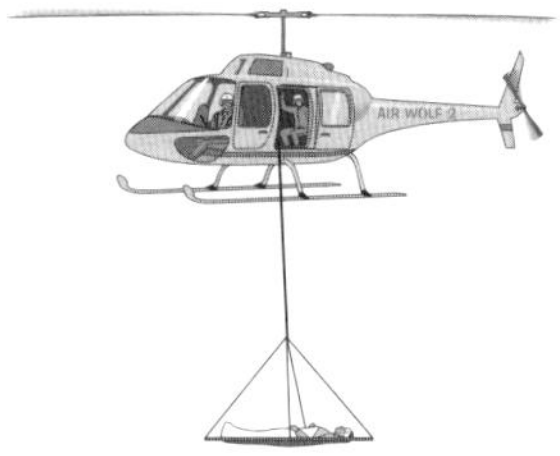

The cable is under

tension / compression.

b)

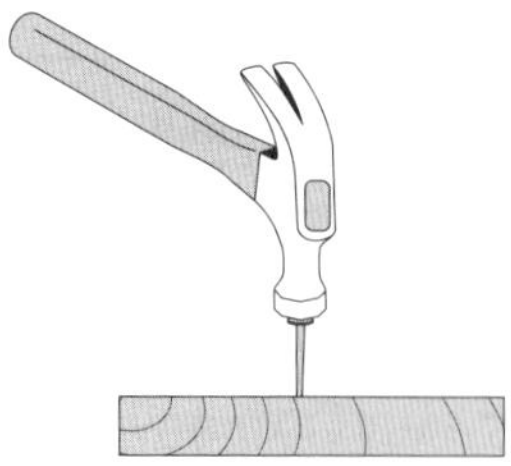

The nail is under

tension / compression.

c)

The clothes inside the suitcase are under

tension / compression.

Q2 Pablo works for a company that makes **climbing ropes**. He's investigating the **mechanical properties** of some different **materials** including their **tensile strength**.

a) What is meant by tensile strength?

....

The table below shows the tensile strengths of four ropes of the same thickness made from different materials.

Rope	Tensile strength (kN)	Density (kg/m^3)
A	15.3	1750
B	5.8	1120
C	7.3	1318
D	10.1	1158

b) i) Which rope has the **greatest** tensile strength?

....

ii) Suggest why this rope might not be suitable for use as a climbing rope.

....

....

iii) Other than tensile strength and density, suggest **one** other mechanical property that Pablo should investigate. Explain why this property is important for climbing ropes.

....

....

Mechanical Properties

Q3 Draw lines to connect each **mechanical property** with the correct **definition**.

Flexibility — how long it takes for a material to wear out

Density — a material's resistance to scratching and indentation

Hardness — how easily a material's shape can be changed

Durability — how much mass there is in a given volume

Q4 Kelly works for a company that designs **pole vault poles**.
The materials used to make the poles have to have certain **properties**.

a) Kelly says that the **density** of the material needs to be as low as possible. Explain why.

....

b) The pole needs to bend and straighten many times without breaking.
What mechanical property should the material have in order to satisfy this requirement?

....

Q5 Saskia is a **sports equipment designer** who is looking for a new material to make **skis**. She is deciding what **properties** the material will need to have.

a) Tick the boxes to show whether the following statements are **true** or **false**.

	True	False
i) The new material will need to be hard.	☐	☐
ii) The new material should be quite brittle.	☐	☐
iii) The new material should be as dense as possible.	☐	☐
iv) The new material should be durable.	☐	☐

b) The flexibility of skis varies. Heavier skiers might find that skis made from a **stiff** material support their weight better than skis made from a flexible material. Suggest why this might be the case.

....

....

Force-Extension Graphs

Q1 For his science coursework Hugo wanted to investigate the **stiffness** of three different materials.

a) In the space below draw a labelled diagram of the apparatus that Hugo could use to measure the stiffness of the different materials.

b) Hugo made sure that all the samples he used were the **same thickness**.
Why did he need to do this?

....

c) A graph of Hugo's results is shown below.

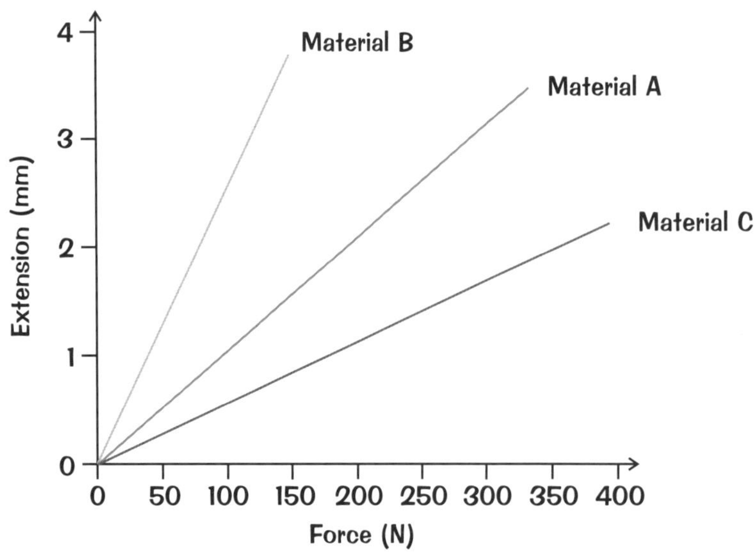

Some stiffness tests are less scientific than others.

Which material had the **lowest** stiffness?

....

Force-Extension Graphs

Q2 Oscar works for the **British Standards Institution**. He is testing a **spring** for a piece of sports equipment before it is given the BSI Kitemark. He has plotted a **force-extension graph** for one of the springs.

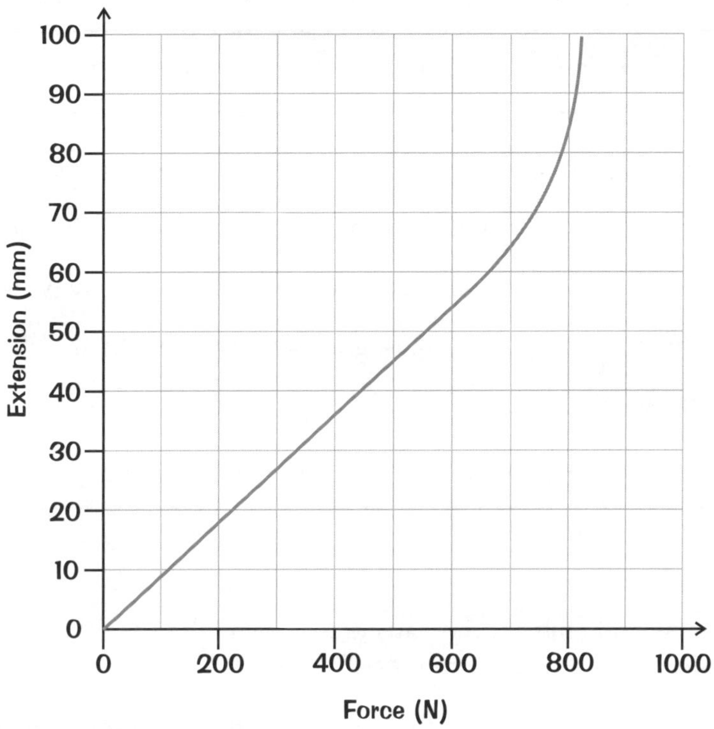

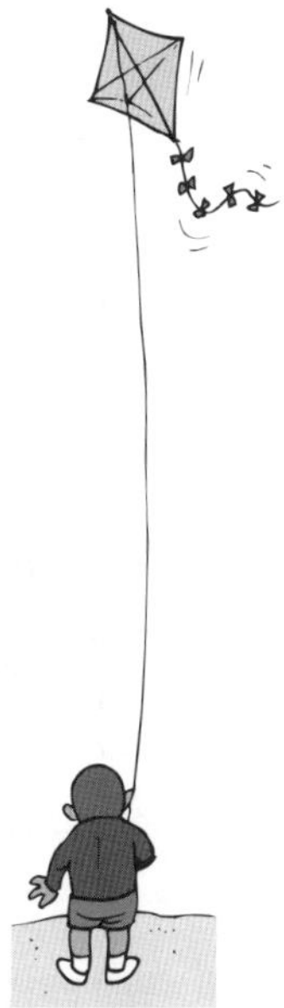

a) To pass the standards test, the spring must extend by more than **42 mm** when a force of **500 N** is applied.

i) What is the extension of the spring when a force of 500 N is applied?

....

ii) Does the spring pass the test?

....

b) Oscar is curious to know how much **energy** is stored in the extended spring.

i) How much does the spring extend in **metres** when a force of 500 N is applied?

....

ii) Use your answer to part **i)** to calculate how much energy is stored in the spring when a force of 500 N is applied. Give your answer in **joules** (**J**).

....

....

Hint: you'll need to work out the area under the graph.

Top Tips: Don't worry about using a calculator to help you with the maths in questions like these — you'll be allowed to take one into the exam. Those examiners must have a heart after all.

Thermal Properties

Q1 Chris is a **material scientist**. She has written the following passage about **thermal conductance** for some school students who are visiting her laboratory.

Use some of the words in the box to fill in the blanks in the passage.
You can use words more than once.

metals heat quickly slowly electrical wood

The ability to conduct thermal or .... energy is called thermal conductance. Materials with a high thermal conductivity include things like .... Materials with a low thermal conductivity include things like polymers. Thermal energy flows through materials with a high thermal conductivity very .... It travels through materials with a low thermal conductivity very ....

Q2 Mark has bought a new **golf club**. Some parts of the golf club are made from **plastic** and other parts are made from **steel**.

When Mark was holding the golf club in the shop, he noticed that the **steel** felt much **colder** than the plastic.

a) Explain why the steel felt colder than the plastic, even though they were at the same temperature.

....

....

b) A diagram of the golf club is shown on the right.

Based on the information above, suggest whether the hand grip or the shaft is most likely to be made of **plastic**.
Explain your answer.

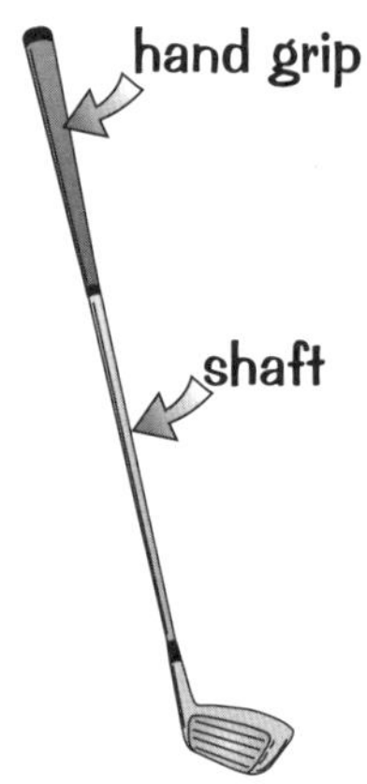

....

....

....

....

Top Tips: You might not think it, but the thermal properties of a material can be dead important when it comes to designing sports equipment. Which is probably why the examiners want you to learn all about the exciting issue of thermal conductivity. Hmm... funny coincidence that.

Thermal Properties

Q3 Dave is a **sportswear designer**. His design team is currently working on several different projects.

The items of sportswear Dave's team are designing are described below.
For each one, tick the correct box to show whether the material it's made from should have a **high** or a **low** thermal conductivity.

a) A wet suit, designed for use in cold water.

high thermal conductivity ☐ low thermal conductivity ☐

b) A sky diving jumpsuit, designed to keep you warm at high altitude.

high thermal conductivity ☐ low thermal conductivity ☐

c) A racing car driver's suit, designed to shield your body from heat in the event of a fire.

high thermal conductivity ☐ low thermal conductivity ☐

Q4 Michelle is a **racing car engineer**. She is investigating the **thermal reflectivity** of different materials in order to make a **heat shield** for the car battery. The heat shield is supposed to wrap around the battery and protect it from the heat produced by the rest of the engine.

a) What is thermal reflectivity?

....

The thermal reflectivities of three different materials are shown in the table below.

Material	Thermal reflectivity
A	0.31
B	0.88
C	0.09

b) **i)** Which of the materials in the table would make the best heat shield? Circle the answer below.

A B C

ii) Explain your answer to part **i)**.

....

....

iii) One of the materials in the table is **aluminium foil**. Suggest which material it could be. Explain your answer.

....

....

Material Properties

Q1 'The Helmet Shack' are trying to develop a new **cycle helmet**. The designers have produced a list of **desirable properties** that the helmet should have.

Draw lines to match the properties to the correct criteria. One has been done for you.

The helmet needs to be very hard-wearing	Aesthetic appeal
The helmet needs to look attractive	Cost
The helmet needs to be quite cheap	Environmental impact
The helmet needs to be made using methods that produce as little pollution as possible	Durability

Q2 Melanie wants to separate some metals, ceramics and polymers based on their **physical properties**.

a) After some research, she finds out that ceramics are **brittle**.

i) Explain what is meant by brittle.

....

ii) Other than being brittle, state **two** other physical properties of ceramics.

1. ....

2. ....

b) Melanie has written descriptions of two materials. Say what types of material A and B are.

Material A is a good conductor of electricity and heat. It is shiny and stiff and can be drawn into wires.

Material B is a good insulator of electricity and heat. It is flexible and can be easily moulded into different shapes.

Material A is a .... Material B is a ....

Q3 Fasto is a company that designs and makes **running shoes**. They need to choose a suitable **metal** to make **spikes** for the bottom of a running shoe.

a) Give **one** property that a metal used for running spikes should have.

....

b) Explain why the property you gave in part **a)** is important in running spikes.

....

More on Material Properties

Q1 A **sports shop** sells some equipment that is made from **composite materials**.

a) What are composite materials?

....

b) Give **two** examples of a composite material.

1. .... 2. ....

Q2 **Tennis racquets** used to be made of **wood**, but today are made from **composite** materials. Here is a picture of a modern tennis racquet and one that people used about 30 years ago.

a) Why are modern composite materials better for making tennis racquets than wood?

....

b) What difference has making tennis racquets out of composite materials, rather than wood, made to the **sporting performance** of tennis players?

....

Q3 Jake is a **racing car designer**. He is researching the **properties** of some **metals** that he is thinking about using for his cars. Below is his table showing the properties of each metal.

Metal	Density (g/cm^3)	Strength (MPa)	Melting point (°C)
Aluminium	2.7	90	660
Cobalt	8.9	225	1495
Steel	7.9	285	825
Titanium	4.5	220	1668

a) Which metal is the strongest? ....

b) Give **one** reason why Jake might use **titanium** in his high performance engines.

....

High performance engines get very hot.

c) Give **one** disadvantage of using **cobalt** in high performance engines.

....

Mixed Questions — Unit 2: Topic 1

Q1 Stephanie **designs sports equipment**. She is making a list of the main **properties** of various materials so that she can choose the best **material** for her designs.

a) Choose from the properties below to complete the table. You can use properties more than once.

brittle good electrical conductor flexible stiff good electrical insulator

good heat conductor good heat insulator ductile shiny

Material	Characteristic properties
Metals	
Ceramic	
Polymers	

b) Stephanie needs a good knowledge of materials and their properties to do her job. What else does she need a good knowledge of? Circle **two** correct answers below.

product standards customer services

product marketing product safety regulations

Q2 **Cermet** is a mixture of a ceramic material and a metal, one of which is embedded in the other. It is **malleable** and a **good heat insulator**. It can be used to coat the outside of engines to provide a heat resistant barrier in sports cars.

a) Is cermet a composite or a polymer?

....

b) Which part of the mixture makes the cermet malleable?

....

c) Explain why a metal or a ceramic by itself wouldn't be suitable for this purpose.

....

....

....

Mixed Questions — Unit 2: Topic 1

Q3 Paul is designing a **javelin**. Javelins need to be made of a **stiff material**. The **stiffer** the material, the **further** the javelin can be thrown.

a) What does it mean when a material is described as stiff?
Tick the box next to the correct answer below.

- ☐ **That the material changes shape easily.**
- ☐ **That the material doesn't deform much under a large load.**
- ☐ **That the material breaks under a large load.**
- ☐ **That the material has a large mass contained in a small volume.**

b) He tests the stiffness of **four** different materials.
The results are shown in the **force-extension graph** below.

Which of the materials shown on the graph would make the best javelin? Explain your answer.

....

....

....

....

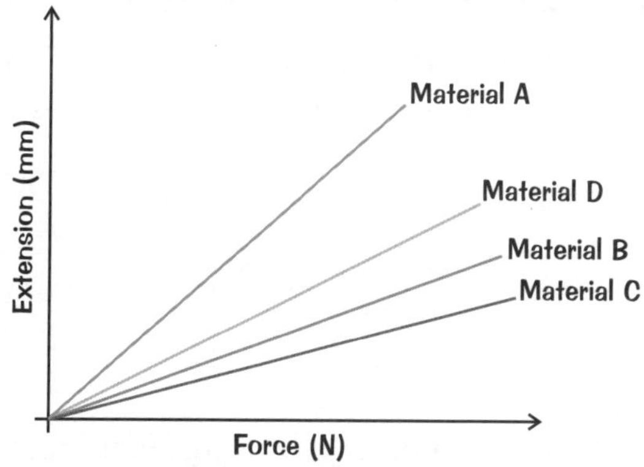

c) Paul doesn't think the javelin he's designing will be stiff enough.
Give **one** way he could increase its stiffness **without** changing the material it is made from.

....

Q4 Jane is a material scientist who is investigating the suitability of ceramic materials as **golf club heads**. She has discovered that ceramic materials are both **hard** and **brittle**.

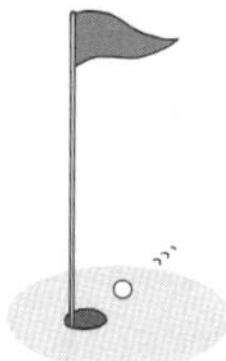

a) Explain what each of these properties means.

i) Hard: ....

ii) Brittle: ....

b) Which of these two properties is an **advantage** of using the material in a golf club head?

....

c) Which is a **disadvantage** of using the material in a golf club head?
Give a reason for your answer.

....

Top Tips: Just think what life would be like without specially chosen materials. Your javelin would break and your golf club head would snap right off. It'd be a great big disaster, I tell you.

Managing Stage and Screen

Q1 **Sound engineers** play an important role in stage and screen.

a) Complete the passage about sound engineers using some of the words from the list.

optics	absorb	seen	equipment	heard	acoustics	works

Sound engineers make sure sound can be ...., is a good quality and safe.
To do this, they need a good knowledge of how sound ....
They need to be able to set-up .... correctly to get the best sound possible.
They also need to know what materials .... or reflect sound to get venue .... right.

b) Describe **one** regulation that sound engineers must follow to keep themselves and the people they work with safe and well.

....

....

Q2 A **film company** is making a new action movie starring Arnie Vin Petrol.

a) The film company has a team of **light engineers** working for them.
Which of the following statements about light engineers are true?
Tick **two** boxes.

- ☐ They must know about the optical properties of different materials.
- ☐ They need to know about the dangers of sound and how to reduce any risks.
- ☐ They don't need to be creative in their role.
- ☐ They only work for film companies.
- ☐ They must be able to use equipment to produce different colours.

b) The film company hires some **visual and special effects experts** to create the movie's special effects. Give **two** technical or scientific skills these experts need to carry out their job.

1. ....

2. ....

Top Tips: Unfortunately this book doesn't contain any visual or special effects — unless you count turning the pages as 3D. Make sure you can describe the scientific and technical skills needed by light engineers, sound engineers and visual and special effects experts. You've also got to know about what regulations they've got to follow to keep themselves and everyone else safe and well.

Managing Light

Q1 Stuart is a **light engineer** for a TV production company.

a) Name **two** sources of light that Stuart might use as part of his job.

1. ....

2. ....

b) Some of the light sources used by Stuart give out ultra-violet (UV) or infra-red (IR) radiation.

i) Give **one** problem caused by each of the following:

UV radiation: ....

IR radiation: ....

ii) Suggest **one** method Stuart could use to reduce the problems caused by UV and IR radiation.

....

Q2 Gabby works as a **light engineer** at a theatre. She is experimenting with **white light** and **filters** to create different coloured light.

a) Gabby sets up a source of **white light**, a **filter** and a **white screen** as shown below.

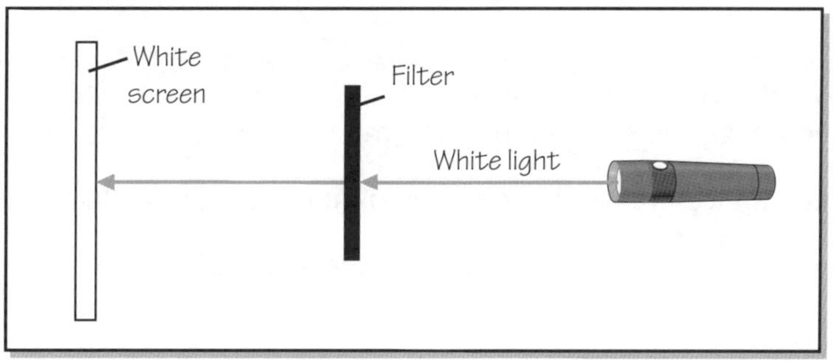

i) If the filter is **blue**, what colour light will hit the screen?

....

ii) Explain your answer to part **i)**. Include the words **absorbs** and **transmits** in your answer.

....

....

b) Circle the correct word in each pair to complete the sentences below.

i) White light appears yellow when **blue** / **red** light is absorbed using a filter.

ii) White light appears **magenta** / **red** when green light is absorbed using a filter.

iii) White light appears cyan when **yellow** / **red** light is absorbed using a filter.

Optical Properties

Q1 Ahmed is sorting marbles into bags, based on their **optical properties**.

a) Draw lines to show which marble should go into which bag.

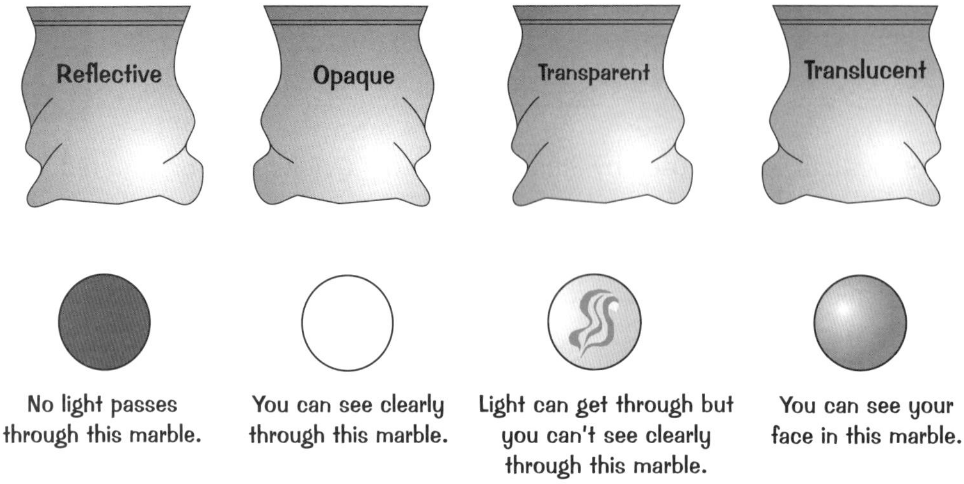

b) Ahmed notices that a ray of light refracts when it enters the transparent marble.
Explain what is meant by **refraction**.

....

....

Q2 Harriet is a special effects expert and is setting up a **plane mirror**. She looks at herself in the mirror. The image she sees is formed from light reflected by the mirror.

a) Complete the diagram to show an incident ray of light being reflected by the mirror.

b) Label the **angle of incidence**, **i**, the **normal**, and the **angle of reflection**, **r**.

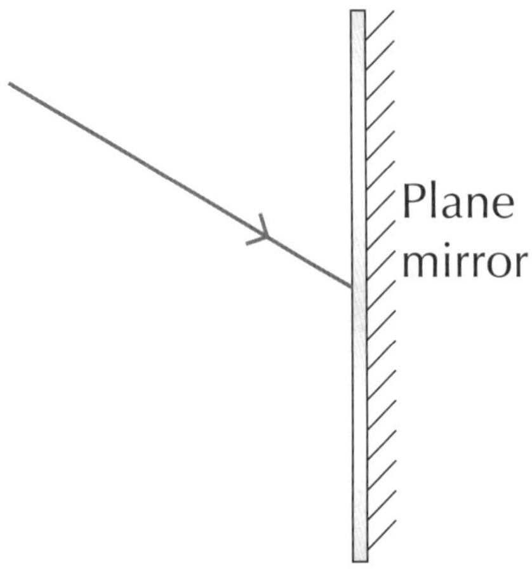

Top Tips: You've really got to get to grips with what the terms transparent, reflective, opaque translucent and refraction mean. It may hurt your head (it hurts mine) but it'll be worth it in the exam.

Optical Properties

Q3 The **optical properties** of **plane mirrors** mean that they can be used to **form images** of objects. This makes them useful to people working in stage and screen.

a) Tick the boxes to show whether the following sentences about the images formed by a **plane mirror** are **true** or **false**.

	True	False
i) The image is as far behind the mirror as the object is in front.	☐	☐
ii) The object is larger than its image.	☐	☐
iii) The image is upside down.	☐	☐
iv) The left and right sides of the object are swapped in the image, i.e. the object's left side becomes its right side in the image.	☐	☐

b) Write out a **correct** version of each of the **false** statements above.

....

....

....

Q4 Mary is using **plane mirrors** in a theatre production. She sets up an object and plane mirror as shown below.

a) On the diagram below, draw the **image** where it would be formed.

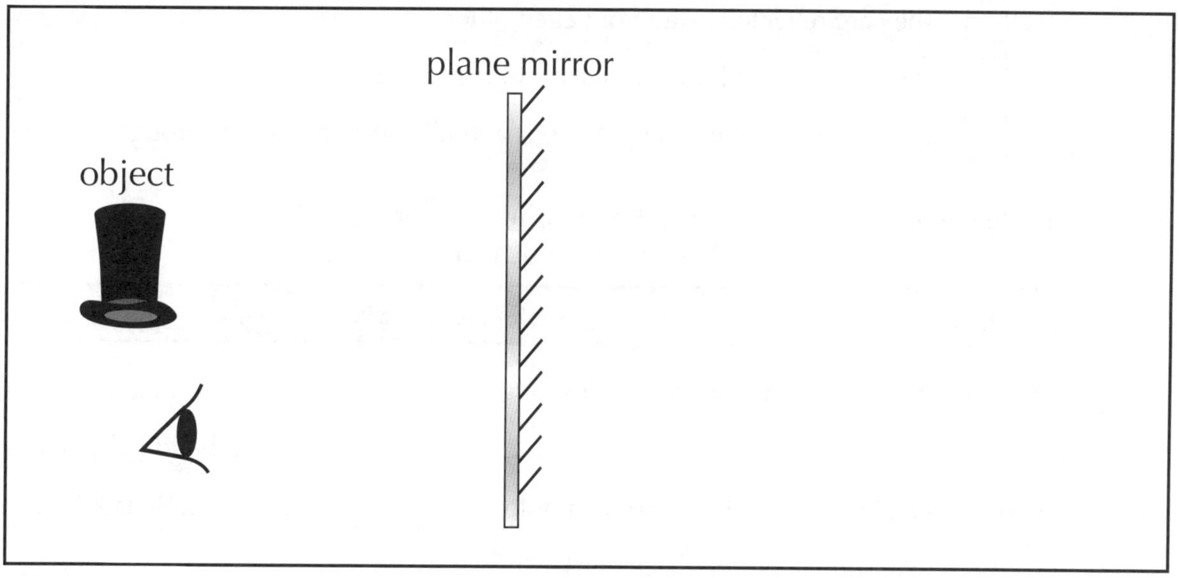

b) **i)** Complete the diagram above by adding **rays** to show how the image of the object is formed by the plane mirror.

ii) Label an **incident ray** and a **reflected ray** on your diagram.

Lenses

Q1 Harry is setting up a **camera** to film a TV show.

Shown below are four different lenses.

A B C D

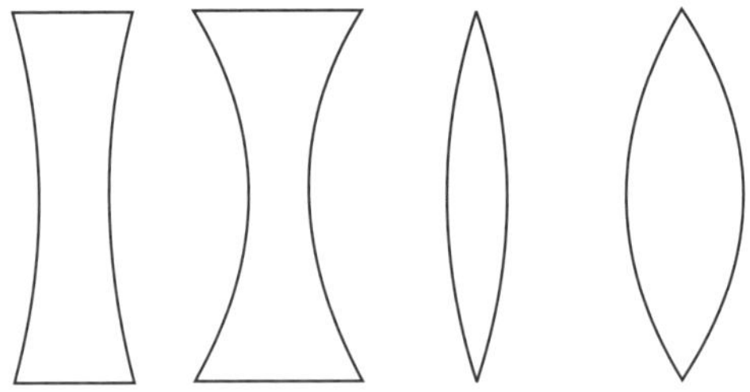

a) **Diverging lenses** are one type of lens.

i) Which **two** of the lenses shown are diverging lenses?

....

ii) Complete the following sentence by circling the correct word(s) in each pair.

Diverging lenses **reflect** / **refract** parallel light rays **away from** / **towards** each other.

b) Harry's camera contains a **converging lens**.
Which of the following describes what happens when **parallel rays of light** hit a converging lens?
Tick **one** box.

- ☐ They are all reflected off the lens.
- ☐ They are refracted away from each other.
- ☐ They are refracted towards each other and meet at a point.
- ☐ The rays are unaffected by the lens and all carry on straight through.

c) Complete the paragraph below about lenses using the words provided.
Words can be used once, more than once or not at all.

glass less fatter closer materials further thinner more

When light travels from air into a lens, it slows down. The .... it slows down the more it bends. Different .... bend light different amounts when light enters them. For example, ... lenses bend light more than some types of plastic lens.

The shape of a lens affects how much it bends light too. The .... or more curved a converging lens is, the .... the image will be formed to the lens.

Lenses and Images

Q1 Mitsuki is a photographer. She takes pictures using a **film camera**.
Label the diagram of Mitsuki's camera using the words provided below.

aperture	lens	focal plane	viewfinder	shutter

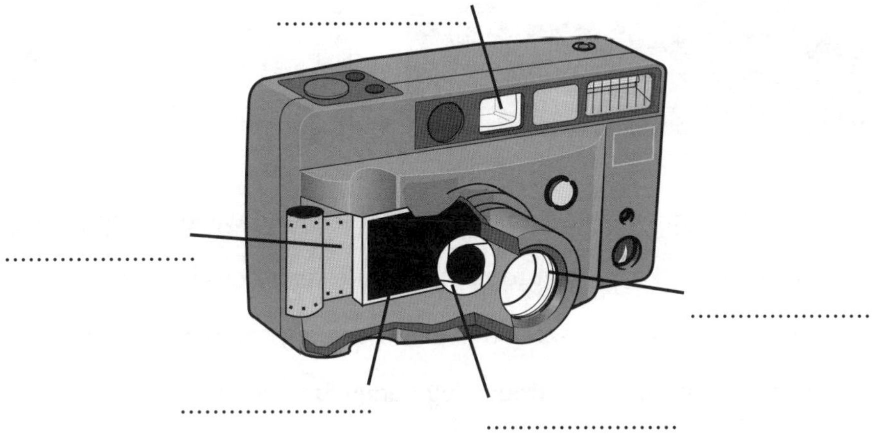

Q2 Pam is training to be a **light engineer**. She is investigating the properties of **images** produced using **converging lens**.

a) Pam sets up an object and a converging lens as shown below. Complete the diagram by adding **rays** to show how the **image** of the object is formed by the converging lens.

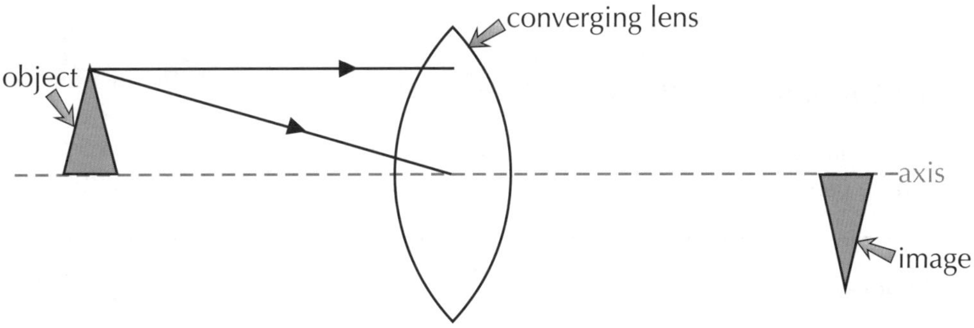

b) Pam replaces the object and lens. Draw a **ray diagram** below to how an image of the object shown is formed by the converging lens.

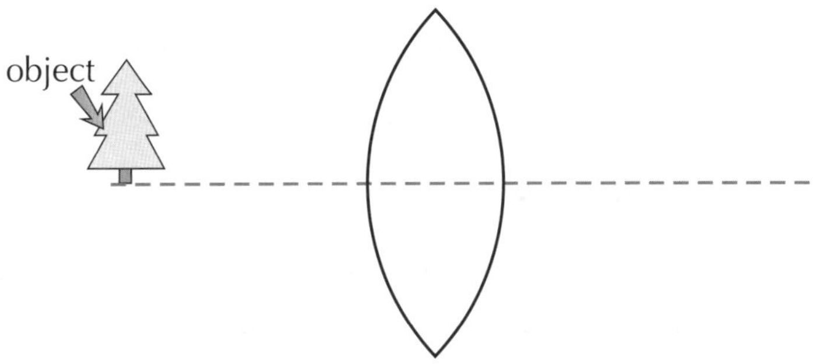

Acoustic Properties

Q1 Kobe is testing a new signal generator. Signal generators can be used to make waves, such as **sound waves**. Kobe connects his signal generator to a **loudspeaker** to see what sound it makes.

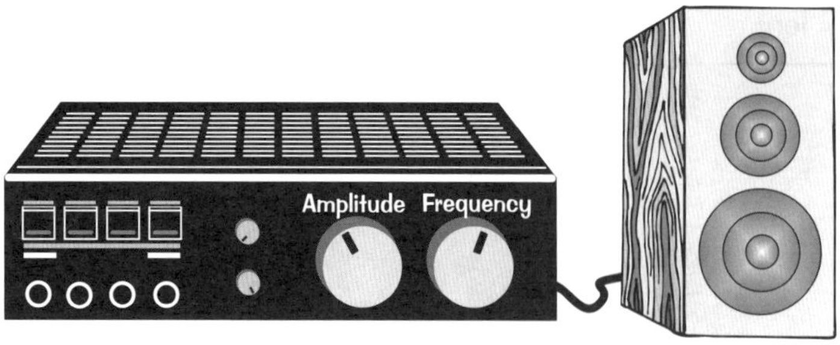

Kobe can adjust the frequency and amplitude of the sound waves using the signal generator.

a) Circle the correct word in each pair to complete the sentences below.

i) The number of vibrations per second is the **frequency** / **amplitude** of a wave.

ii) The size of the vibrations is the **frequency** / **amplitude** of a wave.

b) Kobe **increased** the frequency by turning the dial on the signal generator.
How did the sound change?

....

c) How could Kobe adjust the properties of the sound waves to make the sound **quieter**?

....

Q2 A **musician** buys a **synthesizer** to use with her **keyboard**.

Synthesizers are electronic devices that can mimic other musical instruments or create new sounds.

Complete the paragraph below using the words provided.
Words can be used once, more than once or not at all.

frequencies louder 3000 Hz amplitude decibels 2000 Hz vibrations quieter

The musician notices that notes with .... of about 2000 Hz sounded much .... than other notes, even though the amplitude of the .... was the same. This is because the human ear is more sensitive to some .... and is most sensitive at .... This means that sounds at this frequency seem .... than other frequencies with the same ....

Acoustic Properties

Q3 John is an **environmental health practitioner**. He has written a leaflet about noise and the **decibel (dB) scale**.

a) Fill in the blanks using the correct numbers from below. Numbers can be used once or not at all.

60	85	20	40	10	130	105

Normal conversations occur at about .... dB. To double the loudness you have to increase the intensity by .... dB. Sound intensities above .... dB can cause temporary hearing loss and intensities above .... dB cause pain.

The leaflet recommends that people wear ear protection if they are exposed to loud noise for a long time.

b) List **two** problems that people could suffer from if they don't follow this advice.

1. ....

2. ....

Q4 An **acoustic engineer** has a piece of equipment which measures the intensity of sound on the **decibel scale**. He thinks that this equipment might be broken. He decides to test the equipment by measuring sounds of known **intensities**.

He plots the following graph.

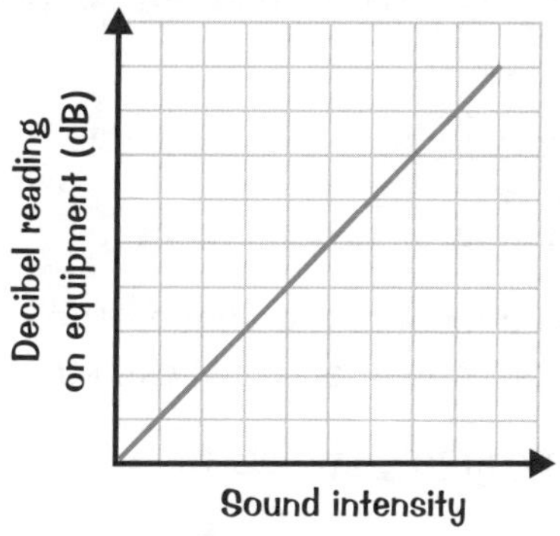

a) Is the equipment working properly? Tick the box to show which statement is correct.

Yes — the graph shows a linear relationship. ☐

No — the graph shows a linear relationship. ☐

b) Circle the correct word(s) to complete the following sentence.

On the decibel scale, an increase in intensity of 20 dB means the sound will be **twice** / **four times** as loud.

Controlling Sound

Q1 Rachel is an environmental health officer. She visits Pauline, who lives near a factory. Pauline has complained that the factory is making too much **noise**. Rachel recommends that Pauline alters some of the materials inside and outside her house, to **reduce** noise levels inside.

a) Circle the correct word in each pair to complete the sentence below.

> To reduce noise levels in Pauline's house she needs materials that **absorb** / **reflect** noise generated inside and **transmit** / **reflect** sounds made outside.

b) Describe **one** thing that Pauline could do to her house to reduce the noise coming from outside.

....

Rachel then visits the factory. She finds that the noise level is dangerously high. She orders the factory to reduce the noise level by isolating the vibrations from the machines.

c) Suggest **two** methods the factory could use to isolate the vibrations.

1. ....

2. ....

Q2 'The Ledge' plays drums for a local rock band.

a) He practises in his **bedroom**. His neighbours have complained about the **noise**. Suggest **two** ways 'The Ledge' could alter his bedroom to reduce the noise level outside.

1. ....

2. ....

b) The Ledge's band are playing at a local music venue. The manager of the venue decides to tell The Ledge all about how the acoustics in the venue are controlled.

Circle the correct word in each pair to complete the sentences below.

i) The venue was built with concrete walls to **reflect** / **absorb** sound.

ii) Fabric panels have been put on the walls to **reflect** / **absorb** sound.

iii) All the doors in the venue are thick to **reduce** / **increase** the amount of sound escaping from the venue.

Top Tips: Reducing noise is all about putting the right materials in the right places. In some places you need materials that absorb sound. In others you need to reflect sound — make sure you get it the right way round. Think about exam halls and why teachers in clicky heels make such a racket...

Managing Sound and Electrics

Q1 Shown below is a diagram of an **electrical circuit** for a lighting system in a theatre.

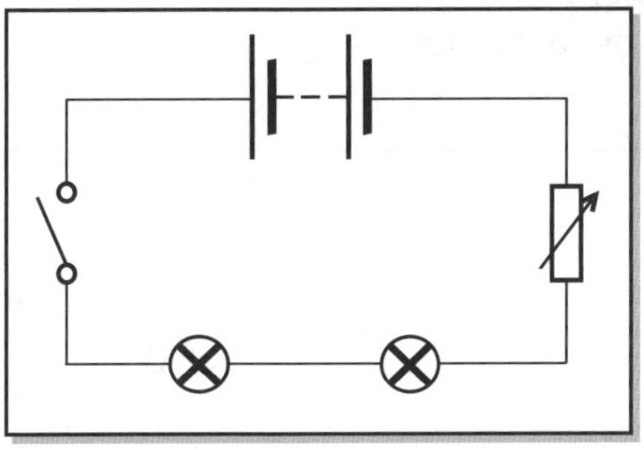

a) Match each **circuit symbol** to the correct label. The first one has been done for you.

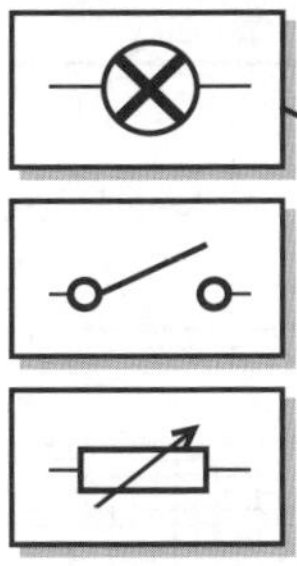

VARIABLE RESISTOR

LAMP

SWITCH

b) Tick the boxes to show whether the following sentences about the electrical circuit are **true** or **false**.

	True	False
i) The switch turns both lamps on or off at the same time.	☐	☐
ii) If one lamp breaks, the other lamp won't be affected.	☐	☐
iii) The brightness of the lamps can be controlled separately.	☐	☐
iv) The variable resistor is used as a dimmer to control the brightness of the lamps.	☐	☐

Q2 Hank is a **sound engineer**. He sets up a simple **sound system** in a venue.

a) Label the diagram of the sound system shown below, using words from the box.

loudspeaker	amplifier	microphone

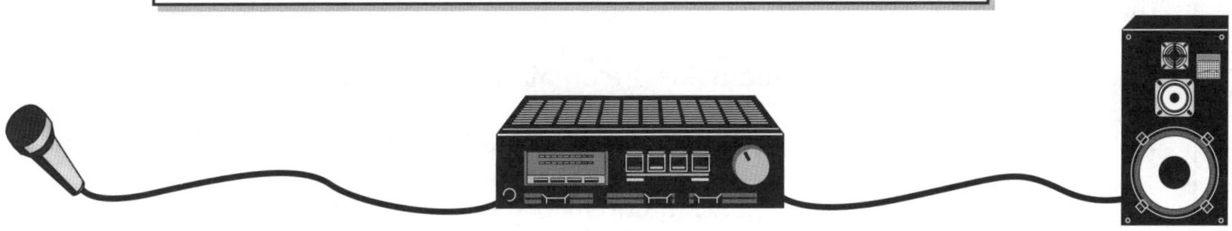

i) .... **ii)** .... **iii)** ....

b) Hank wants to avoid his sound system giving out any **howl**.

Howl is a horrible loud sound, that hurts your ears.

i) Describe how howl happens in a sound system.

....

....

ii) Suggest **one** way in which Hank could set-up the sound system to avoid howl.

....

Managing Indoor Venues

Q1 Kevin is the manager of an **indoor music venue**.

a) Below is a **schematic diagram** of part of the music venue.
Add labels to the diagram to show any sources of **heat** or **ventilation**.
One has been done for you.

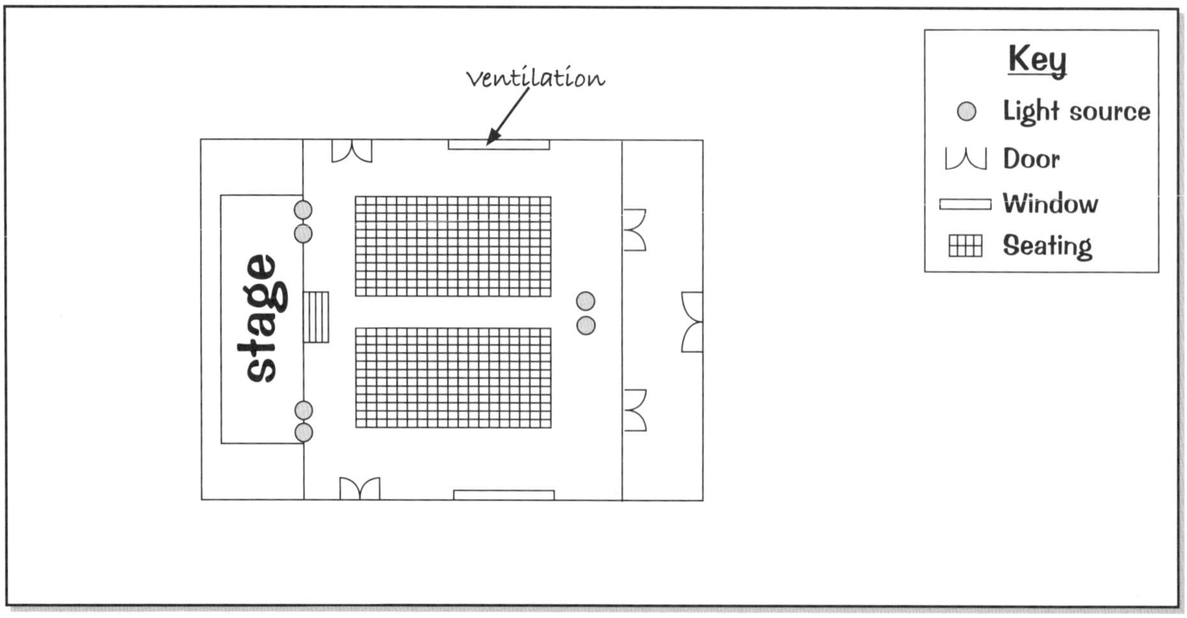

b) The music venue must have certain **health and safety procedures** in place.
Complete the passage about the procedures using words from the list. Use each word only once.

practice	more	purpose	people	time	emergency

In an ...., everyone in the music venue may need to be evacuated. The venue must have procedures in place to make this easy to do. Venues will have .... evacuations, where an alarm is set off on .... This shows how long it takes everyone to evacuate the building — this is called the evacuation .... It can also show problems with .... flow — how people move round a building. To improve any problems .... exits might be put in or people may be told to leave by certain exits.

c) The music venue must also have certain health and safety **features** by law.
Give **three** things that the venue must have to obey these laws.

1. ....

2. ....

3. ....

Mixed Questions — Unit 2: Topic 2

Q1 Sly is a **special effects expert** at a film studio.
He carries out a small, controlled explosion to be used in a film.

a) He uses a **decibel meter** to measure the noise level from his explosion from a safe distance.

i) The noise level is enough to cause **temporary hearing loss** but not enough to cause pain.
What was the reading on Sly's decibel meter? Circle the correct answer.

40 dB   75 dB   120 dB

ii) What would happen to the **loudness** of the sound if it **increased** by **10 dB**?
Tick **one** box.

It would halve. ☐   It would double. ☐   It would triple. ☐

b) The explosion is filmed using a camera containing a **converging lens**.

i) Complete the sentence the below by circling the correct word in each pair.

Lenses are made from **glass** / **copper** because it's **opaque** / **transparent**.

ii) Draw lines to complete the ray diagram for the converging lens below.

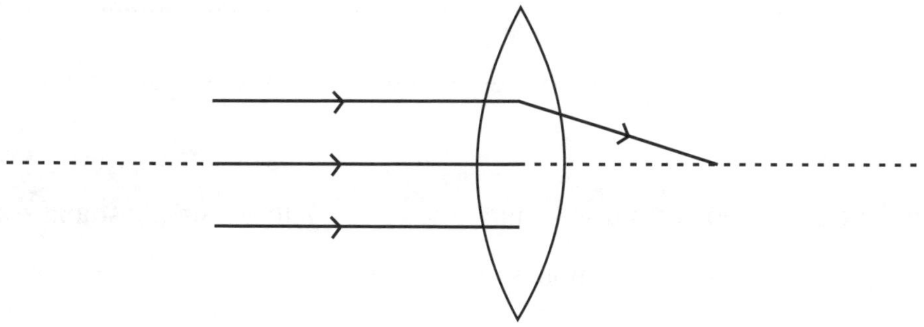

iii) Suggest **one** way in which you could change the lens so that it brings the rays together at a point **closer** to the lens.

....

c) The film studio is located near homes and offices.
Suggest **three** methods which could help reduce the amount of sound escaping from the film studio and reaching the surrounding areas.

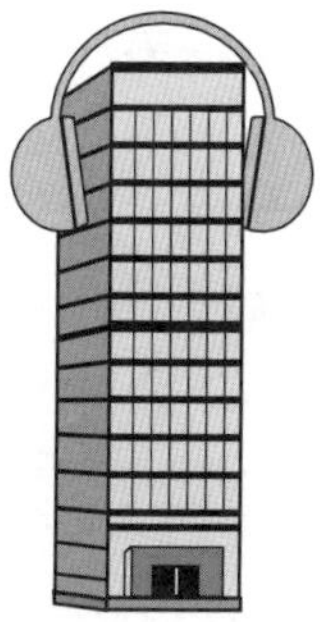

1. ....

2. ....

3. ....

Mixed Questions — Unit 2: Topic 2

Q2 Zofia is a **light engineer** for a theatre company.

a) Zofia has a **white light** source.

i) Describe how she could create **green** light using the white light source.

....

ii) What colour must be removed from white light to make it appear **cyan**?
Tick **one** box.

cyan ☐ red ☐ blue ☐ green ☐

b) Zofia is working with a **translucent** material. What does it mean if something is translucent?
Tick **one** box.

☐ Light cannot pass through it.

☐ Light can pass through it, but you can't see through it clearly.

☐ Most of the light falling on it reflects back off it.

c) Zofia must follow health and safety regulations when carrying out her work.
Suggest **two** things she must do to follow these regulations.

1. ....

2. ....

Q3 Gary's band are setting up at a music venue. They put together a **simple sound system**.

a) Name **three** parts that make up a simple sound system.

1. ....

2. ....

3. ....

b) Gary plays two notes on his guitar. Note **A** has a **higher pitch** than note **B**.
Which note has the **higher frequency**? Tick **one** box.

Note A ☐ Note B ☐

c) During the gig, the fire alarm goes off. The fire alarm makes a sound at a frequency of **2000 Hz**.
Suggest why a frequency of 2000 Hz is used.

....

....

Agriculture in the UK

Q1 Sanjay is a student doing a report on **food production** in the UK.

a) Sanjay starts by researching food products that come from crops. Give the names of **two** crops **and** an example of a food product that each crop is used to produce.

1. Crop .... Food product ....

2. Crop .... Food product ....

b) In his report, Sanjay writes about the way biotechnology is used in food production.

i) Circle the correct word in each pair to complete the sentence below.

> Biotechnology includes the use of **microorganisms** / **crops** such as **chymosin** / **yeast** during the processing and production of food.

ii) Biotechnology is used to make cheese from milk. Give **one** other use of biotechnology in food production.

....

Q2 Marianne is a vet. She specialises in **dairy cows**. The number of cows she has to see has changed over recent years.

a) What is the main product from dairy cows?

....

The table below shows the number of dairy cows in the UK recorded over five years.

Year	Number of dairy cows (thousands)
2007	1954
2008	1909
2009	1857
2010	1847
2011	1814

b) What happened to the number of dairy cows in the UK between 2007 and 2011? Use data from the table in your answer.

....

....

....

c) i) Vets like Marianne were needed much less in 2009 than they were in 2008. Work out the change in the number of dairy cows in the UK over this period.

....

ii) Use your answer from part **i)** to work out the percentage change in the number of dairy cows between 2008 and 2009.

....

....

$$\text{percentage change} = \frac{\text{original value} - \text{new value}}{\text{original value}} \times 100$$

Regulating Agriculture and Food

Q1 **Milkmen** are involved in the **chain of food production**.
They **deliver** fresh milk to customers' homes every morning.

a) What is meant by the **chain of food production**?

....

b) Complete the paragraph on the chain of milk production using the words given below.

delivers   dairy   transported   stored   processed   pasteurising

.... cattle are milked every day on farms. The milk is .... from farms to a dairy for processing. This includes .... The .... milk is sent to local centres where it may be .... until it's needed. The milkman collects the milk from the distribution centre and .... it to his customers.

Q2 Tasty Tea is a specialist tea company that produces flavoured tea bags.
The tea is **processed** in Cumbria from **tea leaves** hand-picked in India.

Draw lines to match each description below to the correct stage in the chain of food production.

Packets of tea bags are sent out to shops for sale	Growing
Tea bushes are grown on plantations in India	Transporting
Packets of tea bags are kept at the Tasty Tea's distribution centre	Processing
The tea leaves are made into packets of flavoured tea bags	Storing
Picked tea leaves are shipped to the UK and driven to Cumbria	Delivering

Q3 Haile works for an organisation that is involved in the **regulation** of agriculture and food production in the UK.

Agriculture is regulated for **three** important reasons.
Tick the three correct boxes below to show what these reasons are.

- For the health and safety of customers ☐
- To protect the rights of shop keepers ☐
- For animal welfare ☐
- To protect homeowners ☐
- To protect supermarket interests ☐
- For the health and safety of workers ☐

More on Regulating Agriculture and Food

Q1 Jeanette is an **enforcement officer**.

a) Complete the paragraph below using the words provided.

rules	environmental health	public	hygiene	monitor	pollution	chain

Enforcement officers make sure .... and regulations are followed by everyone who works in the .... of food production. This helps to protect the health and safety of the .... Factory inspectors .... workplaces and make sure people are abiding by safety rules. .... officers visit places where food is produced or served to make sure that good health and .... practices are being followed. They also help to protect the environment, e.g. by measuring .... levels.

b) Some enforcement officers are **food technologists**.
Describe **one** thing a food technologist does.

....

c) Some enforcement officers have to test the **quality** of food being produced.
Why is it important that the quality of food is tested?

....

Q2 Milktastic make **flavoured milkshakes** for UK supermarkets. They are testing a new ingredient that should **reduce the growth rate** of any **bacteria** in the milkshake.

They monitor the amount of bacteria present in a sample of milkshake every day for a week. The results are shown opposite.

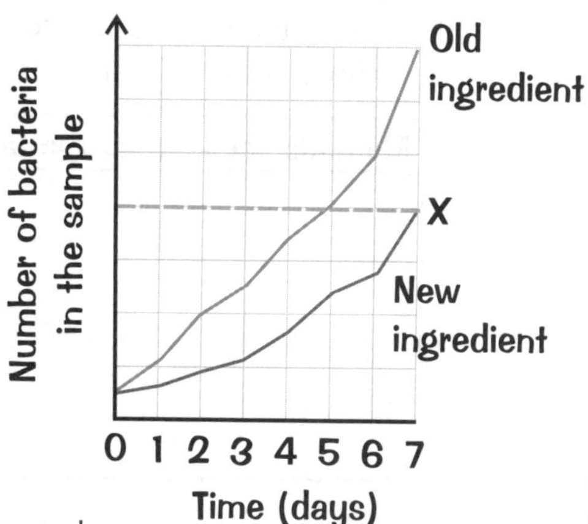

a) Does the new ingredient work?

....

b) Line X shows the number of bacteria that would be regarded as **unsafe**.
After how many days would milkshake with the new ingredient be unsafe? ....

c) Explain why it's important that the safety of the milkshake is tested.

....

Organic and Inorganic Farming of Wheat

Q1 Members of the **Environment Matters to Us (EMU)** are protesting about the use of **artificial chemicals** on local wheat farms.

a) Tick the correct boxes to show whether each statement about artificial chemicals is **true** or **false**.

	True	False
i) Herbicides are chemicals that kill fungi.	☐	☐
ii) Fertilisers stop pests from eating wheat plants.	☐	☐
iii) Insecticides kill insect pests.	☐	☐
iv) Using herbicides in wheat fields reduces the wheat's competition for resources.	☐	☐
v) Using chemicals to kill insect pests means that wheat plants can grow bigger.	☐	☐

b) Give **two** problems related to the use of artificial chemicals, which may have caused members of EMU to protest.

1. ....

2. ....

Q2 Gerrard has taken over an old **wheat farm** in the countryside.

a) Gerrard needs to check his **soil conditions** are right before he plants any new wheat seeds. Explain why he should test the **pH**, **water** and **nutrient** levels in the soil.

i) pH ....

ii) Water ....

iii) Nutrients ....

b) Gerrard can't decide whether he wants to be an **organic** or an **inorganic** farmer. Complete the table below to show **three** farming methods used by organic farmers and **three** farming methods used by inorganic farmers.

Methods used by organic farmers	Methods used by inorganic farmers
1.	1.
2.	2.
3.	3.

Top Tips: All wheat farmers want to grow as much healthy wheat as possible, but organic farmers and inorganic farmers use different methods to do this. Make sure you know the differences between the two farming methods, as well as the benefits and risks of using artificial chemicals.

Wheat Production

Q1 Benjamin has to do a presentation on the **stages** involved in **wheat production** as part of his agriculture course.

a) He has made some notes to help him with the presentation. Some of his notes are shown below. Complete the sentences by circling the correct word in each pair.

> First of all the soil needs to be **sowed / ploughed** to prepare it for growing wheat. Next the wheat seeds need to be **sowed / stored**. When the wheat has grown and is ready to be collected it's **harvested / ploughed**. The wheat is then **dried / watered** and stored until it's ready to be used.

b) At the presentation, a person in the audience asked Benjamin the following question:

"At what point in the wheat production process is a farmer most likely to use chemicals such as fertilisers and pesticides?"

Suggest what Benjamin's reply may have been.

....

....

Q2 Mrs Gilbert manages a **flour mill**. She's been calling different farmers to ask about the **wheat** she can buy from them. The notes she has made are shown below.

Farmer	Type of Wheat	Extra notes
Mrs White	Durum	....
Mr Brown	Bread	....
Mrs Green	....	planted in October
Mr Black	....	planted in March

a) Does Mrs Green grow **spring wheat** or **winter wheat**? How can you tell?

....

b) Mrs Gilbert wants to produce flour to sell to a company that makes **pasta**. Which farmer should she buy wheat from?

....

c) Explain a feature of **bread wheat** that makes it good for making bread.

....

More on Wheat Production

Q1 Erik is a **farmer**. This year he's going to plant some wheat, which he has never grown before. A local seed supplier sends him some information about three different types of **seed**. The information is shown on the right.

Seed type	% germination rate
A	75
B	78
C	84

a) Look at the information in the table. What does **percentage (%) germination rate** mean?

....

b) Erik wants to produce the greatest number of wheat plants from the fewest number of seeds. Which seed type should he buy?

....

c) A friend of Erik's gives him **100 seeds** of **type A** to try. How many wheat plants can Erik expect to grow from these seeds? Circle the correct answer below.

100 75 175 25

Q2 Bruce is a farmer. Every year he works out the **yield** of each of his crops.

a) To work out his wheat yield, Bruce first needs to find the **dry mass** of his wheat. What is meant by the 'dry mass' of the wheat?

....

b) Bruce takes **500 g** of wheat from his field and works out it has a dry mass of **350 g**. Calculate the **percentage dry mass** of his wheat this year.

....

....

$$\text{percentage dry mass} = \frac{\text{dry mass}}{\text{original mass}} \times 100$$

c) i) Bruce uses **8 hectares** of land to grow wheat. Last year he knew that one hectare of his land produced **7.5 tonnes** of wheat. How much wheat did he produce on his land last year? Circle the correct answer below.

15.5 tonnes 60 tonnes 56 tonnes

ii) Last year Bruce's wheat had a percentage dry mass of 80%. Calculate the **total dry mass** of wheat he produced on his land last year.

You'll need to use your answer to part c) i) here.

....

....

Top Tips: If you struggle with calculations like these, it can be tempting to just skip over them (possibly whilst whistling a jolly tune). But don't. The more you practise calculations, the easier you'll start to find them. Which is why there are some on the next page. You'll thank me come the exam.

More on Wheat Production

Q3 Sheila is a wheat farmer with **10 hectares** of land. This year she produced **45 tonnes** of dry wheat from her land. She has asked some other farmers to work out how much dry wheat they produce from 10 hectares of land. Their results are shown on the bar chart below.

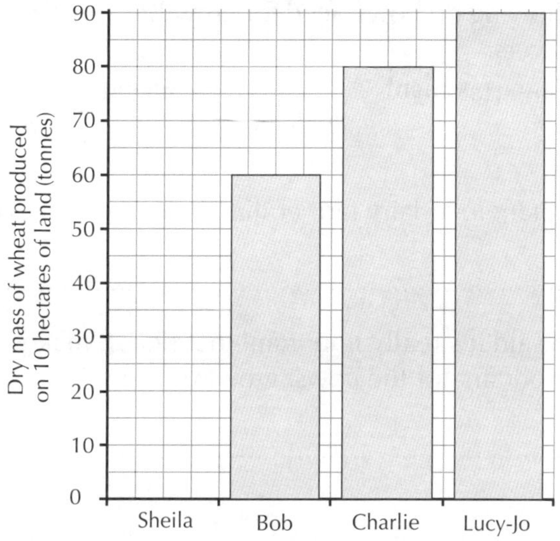

a) Complete the bar chart by adding Sheila's results.

b) How much dry wheat did Bob produce from 10 hectares of land? ....

c) **i)** How much dry wheat did Lucy-Jo produce from **1 hectare** of land?

....

ii) Lucy-Jo has **35 hectares** of land. Use your answer to part **i)** to calculate her **total wheat yield**.

....

....

d) Sheila thinks she might be able to grow more wheat if she uses a different fertiliser. The information on the fertiliser she's thinking of trying says she needs to use **11 litres** of **undiluted fertiliser** per hectare of land.

i) Calculate how many litres of undiluted fertiliser she needs to cover her land.

....

ii) Each litre of fertiliser needs diluting in **20 litres** of water. Using your answer from part **i)**, calculate how many litres of water Sheila will need to add to the fertiliser to cover her land.

....

iii) Charlie has just fertilised his land. He has **38 litres** left over of the **undiluted fertiliser** Sheila has been looking at. He has offered to give it to Sheila. Calculate how much of her land Sheila can cover with 38 litres of undiluted fertiliser.

....

....

Rearing Cattle for Milk

Q1 Keiran took over his grandparent's **dairy farm** three years ago.

a) Before he took over, Keiran's grandad gave him some advice on the things that cows need in order to grow.

i) Which **four** of the following do cows need for growth? Circle the correct answers.

warmth shelter entertainment sunlight company food water

ii) Explain why it's important to a dairy farmer that their cows get everything they need to grow.

....

iii) Keiran's grandad also said it's really important that Keiran makes sure the cows are **healthy**. Explain why this is important for the cows' growth.

....

....

b) Keiran shows his grandad some information on the milk yield of the cows over the past three years. The information is shown in the table on the right.

	Average milk yield per cow (litres)
1st year	7500
2nd year	7300
3rd year	7000

Do you think Keiran's grandad will be pleased with the way Keiran is running the farm based on this information? Explain your answer.

....

....

Q2 George is at a cattle market looking for some **new calves** for his **dairy farm**. He is looking for calves with the **best characteristics** for producing milk.

Give **three** characteristics he might be looking for in his new calves.

1. ....

2. ....

3. ....

Top Tips: Dairy farmers can be pretty picky about their cows. You need to know how they select the cows they want for their farm and how they help them to grow once they've got them.

Breeding Cattle

Q1 Christopher owns a **dairy farm**. He wants to **artificially inseminate** some of his cows.

a) Use the words in the list to complete the passage below about artificial insemination.

fertilisation | an egg | the best | milk | pipette | temperature | frozen

The first step in artificial insemination is the selection of animals with .... characteristics, e.g. high .... yields. The sperm is collected in a device that keeps it at the right .... The sperm is checked for quality and is stored in plastic straws, which can be .... for later use. To inseminate the female a long .... is used to insert the contents of the straw.
It's important to inseminate the female at the right time, just as she is about to release ...., to increase the chances of ....

b) Christopher receives the following information on available sperm stocks.

Bull	Fertility level	Health
A	High	Average
B	High	Good
C	Medium	Good

Fertility level is the likelihood that the bull's sperm will fertilise an egg.

Which bull's sperm should Christopher buy? Circle the correct answer below.

C   A   B

c) Christopher has chosen to use artificial insemination because it has advantages over natural mating.

i) One advantage is that artificial insemination is **cheaper** than natural mating. Explain why this is.

....

....

ii) Other than cost, give **two** advantages of artificial insemination over natural mating.

1. ....

2. ....

Breeding Cattle

Q2 Jeremy is a dairy farmer. He uses **selective breeding** to breed his cattle.

a) Use the words in the list to complete the paragraph below about selective breeding. You can use each word once or not at all.

bulls   quality   weight   lots of   cows   live   breed

Selective breeding is when humans choose the animals that are going to .... according to what we want from them. Dairy farmers selectively breed cattle to get .... that produce .... milk, and milk that is of a good ....

b) Number the sentences below to show the stages of selective breeding in the correct order. The first one has been done for you.

- ☐ Breed them with each other.
- ☐ Select the best offspring.
- ☐ Continue the process over many generations.
- ☐ Combine with the best you already have and breed again.
- 1 Select individuals with the best characteristics.

Q3 Clara is looking for some new cattle to breed on her **dairy farm**. She's gathered information on **three breeds of cow** and **three breeds of bull** as shown below.

a) Which breeds of cow and bull do you think Clara should choose to breed together? Explain your choices.

....

....

....

....

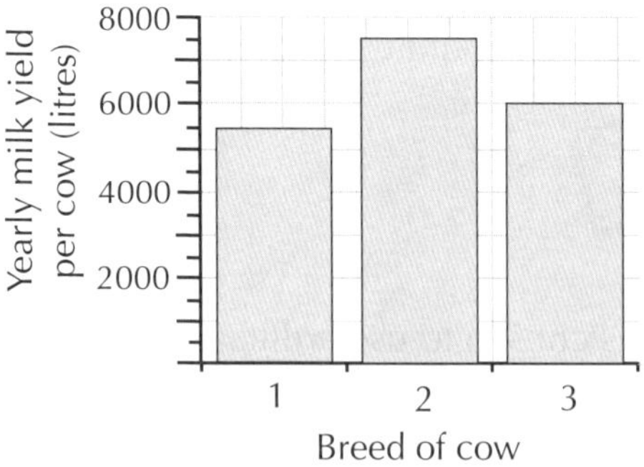

Breed of bull	Quality of sperm
1	Good
2	Average
3	Poor

b) Explain why it's important that Clara continues the selective breeding process over several generations.

....

c) Clara is told about another breed of cow (breed 4) with a milk yield 50% higher than breed 1. Work out the yearly milk yield of a cow from breed 4.

Start by working out 50% of breed 1's milk yield.

....

....

Processing Milk

Q1 Tariq owns a small corner shop. One of his customers has noticed that Tariq sells both **pasteurised** and **UHT** milk.

a) Use the words in the list to complete the passage below about pasteurisation. You can use each word once or not at all.

ill cooling bacteria enzymes heating damage kill

Pasteurisation involves .... a substance, then .... it.

This is done to .... the most harmful ...., so the

product shouldn't make you ....

b) Describe what happens during UHT processing.

....

....

c) The customer wants to buy the milk that will last the longest.
Which type of milk should Tariq sell to the customer? Circle the correct answer below.

UHT pasteurised

Q2 Dan is investigating how **temperature** affects the **growth of bacteria**. He puts **milk** into three test tubes and adds **resazurin** dye. He stores each tube at either 5 °C, 15 °C or 30 °C for 24 hours.

Resazurin dye changes colour according to the number of microorganisms present in the milk sample. These colour changes are shown in the chart below.

blue → lilac → mauve → pink → colourless

Least microorganisms Most microorganisms

a) Explain why the Resazurin test is used to test the freshness of milk.

....

....

b) The table on the right shows Dan's results after 0, 12 and 24 hours.

Time (hours)	0	12	24
Tube 1	Blue	Mauve	Colourless
Tube 2	Blue	Lilac	Mauve
Tube 3	Blue	Blue	Blue

i) Suggest which test tube Dan stored at 30 °C.

....

ii) Explain your answer to part **i)**.

....

....

Bacteria grow faster at higher temperatures.

Microorganisms — Uses and Dangers

Q1 Amy works in **food production**. She is developing new ways of using **microorganisms** in food production.

a) Which of the following are microorganisms? Circle **three** correct answers.

viruses worms fleas antigens yeasts bacteria

b) Give **one** example of a type of alcohol, a food product and an enzyme that are made using microorganisms.

i) Alcohol ....

ii) Food product ....

iii) Enzyme ....

Q2 Amar tests some samples from a **food factory** for the presence of **microorganisms** that can cause **food spoilage**.

a) Explain how microorganisms can cause food spoilage.

....

....

b) Amar uses **aseptic techniques** when testing his samples.
Why does he use aseptic techniques? Underline the correct statement.

To make sure things are measured correctly. To kill any microorganisms in his sample. To prevent contamination.

c) Circle the correct word to complete the following sentence.

All / **some** / **no** microorganisms cause disease.

Q3 **Scientists** from the Food Standards Agency are investigating a case of **food poisoning** caused by some meat. They have collected some samples of meat from the **abattoir**, the **butcher** and the **food** that caused the food poisoning.

An abattoir is a place where animals are killed for their meat.

They measure the numbers of microorganisms in each sample by counting each cluster of cells that has grown. The results are shown on the right.

Abattoir Butcher Food

a) How many clusters of microorganisms did the sample collected from the food contain?

....

b) What might explain the growth of microorganisms in the food sample?
Tick the correct answer.

The meat was stored incorrectly after it was bought from the butchers. ☐

The meat was stored incorrectly at the abattoir. ☐

The meat wasn't cooked before it was eaten. ☐

Products from Microorganisms

Q1 **Yeast** is a microorganism that can be used to make a variety of **food products**.

a) Circle the correct word in each pair to complete the following passage about microorganisms.

> Microorganisms use **photosynthesis / respiration** to release **energy / oxygen** from **sugars / salts**. This process is also known as **distillation / fermentation**.

b) **Anaerobic** fermentation by yeast can be used to make alcoholic drinks. Use the words given below to complete the equation for anaerobic respiration in yeast. Words can be used once or not at all.

carbon dioxide   water   lactic acid   ethanol   sugar   glucose

.... → .... + ...

c) Name another useful product that can be made using anaerobic respiration in yeast.

....

Q2 Some **vegetarians** eat a meat substitute made from **mycoprotein**.

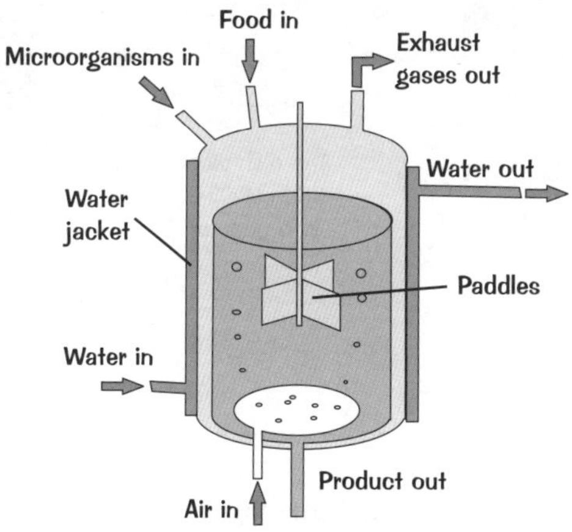

The diagram opposite shows a fermenter that can be used for producing mycoprotein. The microorganisms respire **aerobically** during mycoprotein production.

a) Explain the purpose of the air supply.

....

....

....

b) What type of microorganism is used to make mycoprotein?

....

c) Write the word equation for aerobic respiration.

....

Top Tips: Remembering equations can be pretty tricky, especially when you have a few similar sounding ones to learn. If you can answer the questions on this page correctly, then you know you've got them sorted. If not, make sure you learn the equations off by heart before the exam.

More Products from Microorganisms

Q1 Chris is learning about the **cheese-making process**.

a) Circle the correct word to complete the sentence below.

Anaerobic fermentation by **bacteria** / **yeast** is used when making cheese.

b) Tick the box to show which statement best describes anaerobic fermentation.

When microorganisms respire in the absence of oxygen. ☐

When microorganisms respire in the presence of oxygen. ☐

c) Write out the word equation for the anaerobic respiration used in cheese making.

....

Q2 **Yogtastic** is a Cornish **yoghurt manufacturer** that wants to increase its national sales by improving its **website**. The owners think that an **explanation** of how yoghurt is made might encourage people to buy their products **online**.

The diagram below shows the stages involved in producing yoghurt.

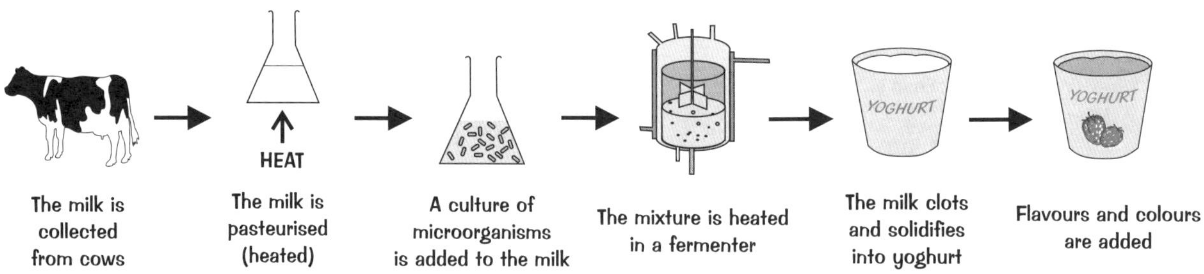

a) Why is the milk **pasteurised**?

....

b) What type of microorganism is added to the milk? Circle the correct answer.

yeast **viruses** **bacteria** **fungi**

c) The microorganisms convert sugar in the milk into lactic acid.

i) What is this process called?

....

ii) Based on this information, is oxygen present in the fermenter?

....

More Products from Microorganisms

Q3 Bruno and his family make **coffee** in Brazil. They have to ferment the coffee beans before they can be dried and processed to sell.

a) Why are coffee beans left to ferment? Tick the correct answer below.

- To soften the mucilage. ☐
- To allow the mucilage to form. ☐
- To harden the mucilage. ☐

The mucilage is a slimy layer that coats coffee beans.

b) Explain how microorganisms present on the coffee beans affect the mucilage.

....

....

Q4 Lei runs a Chinese restaurant. She spends a lot of money on buying **soya sauce**. She's looking into how it's made to see if she could make it more cheaply herself.

a) What is soya sauce?

....

b) What happens first in soya sauce production? Tick the correct answer below.

- ☐ The liquid is drained off the soya beans to produce the soya sauce.
- ☐ Enzymes are added to soya beans.
- ☐ Microorganisms are added to soya beans.

c) **Fermentation** needs to take place during soya sauce production. Why is this? Circle the correct answer below.

So that microorganisms produce hormones.

So that microorganisms produce enzymes.

So that microorganisms increase the pH of the soya beans.

d) Explain why the soya beans are **soft** after fermentation.

....

....

Growth of Microorganisms

Q1 Tristan is a microbiologist. In a recent experiment he studied the **growth** of a **culture of bacteria** over time. He used his findings to draw the chart below.

a) The growth phases of the bacterial culture are labelled A – D on the chart. Draw lines to match each growth phases to its correct name below.

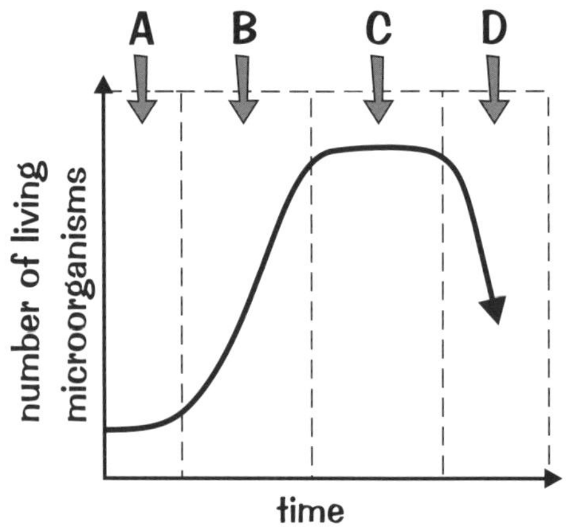

A	exponential growth phase
B	senescence (death phase)
C	lag phase
D	stationary phase

b) During which phase are the conditions best for bacterial growth? ....

c) Explain what happens to the number of bacteria during the growth phase labelled '**D**' on the chart.

....

....

....

Q2 Rose is growing bacteria. At 30 °C a single bacterium reproduces **once** every **15 minutes**.

Rose leaves **ten** bacteria to reproduce for 60 minutes at 30 °C.

You'll need to use a calculator to help you with this question.

a) How many times will the bacteria reproduce in 60 minutes?

....

b) How many bacteria will Rose have at the end of 60 minutes?

....

....

Q3 Microorganisms can be grown in **batch** or **continuous cultures**.

Complete the table by giving **one** advantage and **one** disadvantage for each of these processes.

	BATCH	CONTINUOUS
Advantage		
Disadvantage		

Bioreactor Conditions

Q1 Alan works for a company that makes **bioreactors**. His job is to test new models of bioreactors before they are sold for use in the food industry.

a) What are bioreactors used for in the food industry?

....

b) Number the following statements (1-3) to show how the conditions inside a bioreactor are monitored.

☐ **Information about the conditions inside the bioreactor is processed by a computer.**

☐ **Information about the conditions inside the bioreactor is displayed by data logging software.**

☐ **Information about the conditions inside the bioreactor is picked up by sensors.**

c) Alan looked at the following graph which shows information about the temperature inside a new bioreactor he was testing.

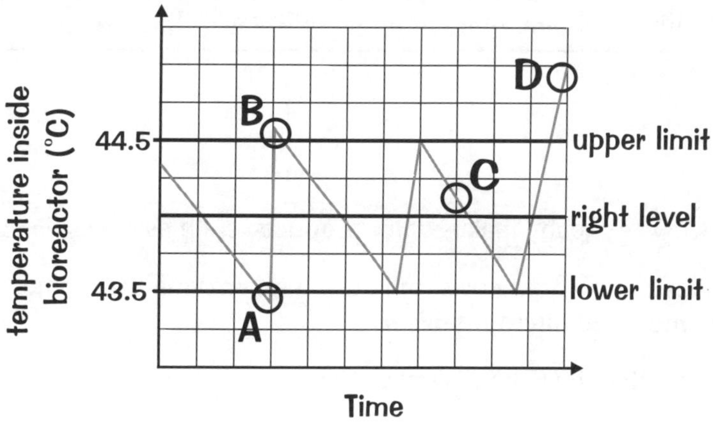

Suggest at which point on the graph (A, B, C or D) the following things happened:

i) Sensors detected the temperature inside the bioreactor was too high. ....

ii) Heaters were triggered to come on. ....

iii) An alarm was triggered to signal there was a fault with the bioreactor. ....

iv) The temperature was within the correct limits. ....

d) Other than temperature, give **one** condition that is controlled in a bioreactor.

....

e) Explain why it's important that the conditions inside a bioreactor are monitored and controlled.

....

....

Genetically Modified Microorganisms

Q1 **Mr Hobbs** is teaching his class about **genetically modified organisms**.

Use the words in the list to complete the passage below.
You may use each word once, more than once or not at all.

proteins, protein material, gene, protein, food, chemical, GM, genes, GB, genetic material

An organism's DNA is also known as its .... A short section of DNA is called a .... Each .... codes for a particular .... in an organism.

We can produce large amounts of useful .... from microorganisms by modifying their DNA. Microorganisms that have been modified in this way are known as .... microorganisms. These microorganisms play an important role in the .... industry.

Q2 The Complacent Cow Company makes **dairy products**, such as **cheese**.

a) The company makes cheese from cows' milk using an **enzyme** that comes from a **genetically modified microorganism**.

i) Name the enzyme that the Complacent Cow Company uses.

....

ii) What type of microorganisms are modified to produce the enzyme? Circle the correct answer below.

fungi   yeasts   bacteria   viruses

b) Other than to make the enzyme used in cheese production, give **one** way that the Complacent Cow Company might use genetically modified microorganisms.

....

....

Top Tips: Genetically modified microorganisms aren't as complicated as they sound. Basically they're just microorganisms that have had their DNA altered. The food industry love them because they can produce loads of useful products that can be used in food production.

Mixed Questions — Unit 2: Topic 3

Q1 Henry works on a small **farm**, picking **cherries**.

Henry picks some cherries and puts them in the farm shop for sale. After three days the cherries that hadn't been sold looked spoiled. The cherries are shown on the right.

a) How can you tell the cherries are spoiled? Tick the one correct answer.

- They are smaller than normal cherries ☐
- You can see the waste products produced by microorganisms ☐
- You can see the visible growth of microorganisms ☐

b) Cherry wine can be made from the cherries using yeast. The yeast respire anaerobically.

i) Name the **two** products of **anaerobic** respiration in yeast.

1. ....

2. ....

ii) Yeast can also respire aerobically. Name the **two** products of **aerobic** respiration in yeast.

1. ....

2. ....

Q2 Francis works in **food production**.

a) She is trying to modify a microorganism so that it will produce a useful enzyme.

i) What is this process called? Circle the correct answer.

mycoprotein modification | respiration | genetic modification | fermentation

ii) Name **one** enzyme that is produced using this method.

....

b) The company Francis works for uses a **batch culture** method to grow microorganisms. Francis thinks they should be using a **continuous culture** method instead.

i) Suggest **one** reason why the company Francis works for uses batch culture rather than continuous culture.

....

ii) Suggest **one** reason why Francis thinks it would be better to swap to a continuous culture method for growing microorganisms.

....

Mixed Questions — Unit 2: Topic 3

Q3 Massive Milk Makers have a factory that **processes milk**.

a) The factory produces **skimmed milk**. Explain how skimmed milk is made from full fat milk.

....

b) **Enforcement officers** sometimes visit Massive Milk Makers.

i) Some of these enforcement officers are **factory inspectors**.
Why might a factory inspector visit the company? Underline **three** correct answers below.

To monitor the level of pollution created by the company.

To make sure the company are sticking to health and safety rules.

To investigate any complaints reported about the company.

To make sure that the milk produced by the company is of a good quality.

To suggest new ways of making milk products to the company.

ii) Name the type of enforcement officer that would **check** the **fat content** of the milk that Massive Milk Makers produce.

....

c) After it has been processed, which stage of the chain of food production would the milk move onto next? Circle the correct answer below.

growing | delivering | storing | transporting

Q4 Farmer Hawk is a **dairy farmer**.

a) In the winter Farmer Hawk's cattle spend a lot of time in a **shelter** to keep them warm. Explain how this may affect the **growth** of the cattle.

....

....

b) When Farmer Hawk breeds her cattle she inserts long pipettes filled with a bull's sperm into her cows. What is this method of breeding called? Circle the correct answer below.

genetic engineering | natural mating | artificial insemination

Mixed Questions — Unit 2: Topic 3

Q5 **Microorganisms** are used to make lots of useful **food products**.

Use the words in the list to complete the passage below.
You may use each word once, more than once or not at all.

cheese	anaerobic	enzymes	sugar
soya sauce	aerobic	lactic acid	genes

.... fermentation in *Lactobaccili* is used to make food, like cheese and yoghurt. In this process, ... is made into ....

.... fermentation in yeast is used to make food products such as yeast extract. In this process, ... is converted into ethanol and carbon dioxide.

Fermentation of microorganisms can also produce useful .... which are used to make food products such as coffee and ....

Q6 Abdullah is an **organic** farmer. He grows **wheat crops** that are processed into flour.

The table on the right gives some data about how much flour can be produced from one bushel of wheat. A bushel is a unit of measurement.

	From one bushel
Mass of wheat (kg)	27
Mass of flour (kg)	19

a) Abdullah's field can produce **37 bushels** of wheat.

i) Calculate the amount of **flour**, in **kg**, that can be produced from one field of wheat.

....

ii) Abdullah dries out the wheat from **one bushel**. It now has a mass of **22 kg**.
Work out the **percentage dry mass** of Abdullah's wheat.

....

b) Abdullah has a friend, John, who's an **inorganic** farmer. He uses a **fungicide** on his wheat crops. John says this makes his wheat crops grow bigger.

i) Explain how fungicides make wheat crops grow bigger.

....

....

ii) Abdullah and John both know that it's important that their wheat plants get enough nutrients.
Give **one** way that each farmer may increase the nutrient content of their soil.

Abdullah ....

John ....

The Chemical Industry

Q1 Joe is a **laboratory technician**. He works for a local chemical plant. Tick the boxes to show whether the following statements about laboratory technicians are **true** or **false**.

		True	False
a)	Laboratory technicians make sure lab equipment works and is safe to use.	☐	☐
b)	Laboratory technicians make product formulations.	☐	☐
c)	Laboratory technicians aren't involved in any testing or analysing of product samples.	☐	☐
d)	The main role of a laboratory technician is to research new chemical products.	☐	☐

Q2 The four people below work in the **chemical industry**.

Draw lines to match each person's job title with the correct description of their role.

Plant manager — Research chemist — Chemical engineer — Finance officer

Manages the chemical plant's money.

Figures out what new products to make and how to make them.

Oversees the daily running of the chemical plant.

Designs the manufacturing process needed to make the product on a large scale.

Q3 A company is deciding where to build its new **chemical plant**. The **two possible sites** for the plant are described below.

Site A
- Located two miles from nearest town and five miles from nearest motorway. Good rail links.
- Close to local reservoir, landfill and power station.
- Several chemical plants already present in area.

Site B
- Rural location. Five miles from nearest town and twenty miles to nearest motorway.
- Plenty of space for a landfill area and power station to be built on site.
- No other chemical plants in local area.

Should the company build their chemical plant at **site A** or **B**? Give **two** reasons for your answer.

Site: .... Reasons: ....

....

....

....

Regulating the Chemical Industry

Q1 The **HSE** is an organisation set up by the UK government. What is the HSE? Circle the correct answer below.

The Hygiene and Safety Executive

The Hearing and Sound Executive

The Health and Safety Experiment

The Health and Safety Executive

Q2 a) Tick the boxes to show whether the following statements about the **HSE** are **true** or **false**.

	True	False
i) The HSE is only concerned with keeping workers safe.	☐	☐
ii) The HSE checks that chemical companies follow the safety rules.	☐	☐
iii) The HSE makes sure that laws relating to the use or manufacture of chemicals are followed.	☐	☐
iv) The HSE makes sure that workers don't have to use dangerous chemicals.	☐	☐

b) Write out a **correct** version of each of the **false** statements above.

....

....

....

Q3 a) Dave is a **HSE inspector**. He has identified some problems at a chemical plant. Draw lines to match each problem described below with the appropriate **action** Dave should take.

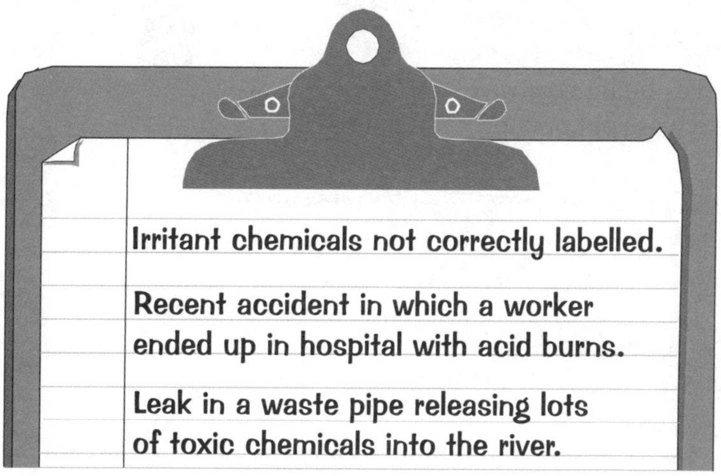

Shut down the plant. Reopen only when the fault has been dealt with satisfactorily.

Investigate circumstances then give appropriate advice to prevent problem happening again.

Advise the company on how to put the fault right.

b) Apart from a chemical plant, give **one** other place where people work with chemicals that Dave might need to inspect.

....

Risk Assessments and Hazchem Symbols

Q1 Nadim works in a **hospital**. He comes across many different types of chemicals, some of them **hazardous**.

a) Fill in the meaning of each hazchem symbol below by choosing the correct label from the box.

corrosive	toxic	irritant	explosive
harmful	highly flammable	oxidising	

i) ....

ii) ....

iii) ....

iv) ....

v) ....

vi) ....

vii) ....

b) Some of the chemicals are labelled as being **corrosive**.
What would happen if one of these was spilt on a person's hands?

....

....

c) Other chemicals are labelled as being **oxidising**.
Explain how they could be dangerous.

....

....

Top Tips: It's pretty important to understand hazchem symbols — not only to pass your exam but also to make sure that you work safely in the lab when you're doing your own experiments.

Risk Assessments and Hazchem Symbols

Q2 The **HSE** has published a leaflet describing five steps to **risk assessment**.

1. Identify hazards.
2. Decide who might be harmed and how.
3. Assess the risk and decide on precautions.
4. Record findings and implement them.
5. Review assessment regularly.

a) Step 3 involves assessing a risk. What are the **two** most important things you should consider when assessing a risk?

1. ....

2. ....

b) Assess the risk involved in the following activities.
Circle whether you think they are low risk, medium risk or high risk.

i) Using bleach, an irritant, to clean a kitchen. **low risk / medium risk / high risk**

ii) Watching fireworks from a distance. **low risk / medium risk / high risk**

iii) Working closely with toxic substances. **low risk / medium risk / high risk**

Q3 Billy Bob is a tanker driver for a **chemical company**. His tank is shown below.

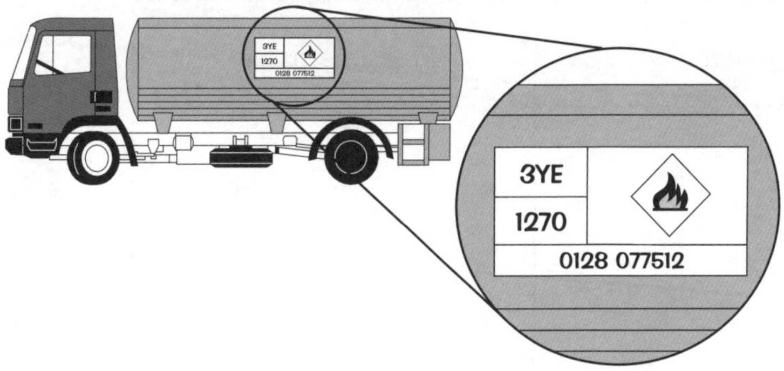

a) Suggest **one** type of chemical that he could be carrying in his tank.

....

b) Explain your answer to part **a)**.

....

....

Industrial Production of Chemicals

Q1 Use some of the words in the box to complete the passage below.

iron	salts	carbon	rocks	metals	acids

Metal ores are .... containing minerals that

.... can be extracted from.

Copper and .... can both be extracted from ores and used to make insoluble and soluble ....

Q2 Some **bulk chemicals**, some **fine chemicals** and their **uses** are given below.

ammonia — fertiliser

quinacridone — paint pigment

phosphoric acid — fertiliser manufacture

tartrazine — food colouring

aspirin — painkiller

sulfuric acid — detergent manufacture

a) Circle the correct word from the pair to complete the following sentence.

A bulk chemical is a chemical that is manufactured on a **large** / **small** scale.

b) Complete the table to show whether each chemical named above is a bulk chemical or fine chemical:

Bulk chemicals	Fine chemicals

Incredible bulk

c) Suggest why fine chemicals are **more expensive** than bulk chemicals.

....

d) Sodium hydroxide is a bulk chemical. Give **two** uses for sodium hydroxide.

1. .... 2. ....

Acids and Alkalis

Q1 Frank is a **food scientist** who works for a drinks manufacturer. He is testing the **pH** of various fizzy drinks.

a) Explain what the **pH** of a substance tells you about it.

....

b) **i)** Frank needs to know the **approximate pH** of a fizzy drink. What could he use to estimate this?

....

ii) Frank is asked to accurately test the pH of another fizzy drink, without using any chemicals. Suggest a way he could do this.

....

c) Frank was asked to test the pH of a fizzy drink and some other liquids. Tick the boxes to show whether the liquids he tested are acidic, alkaline or neutral.

	acidic	neutral	alkaline
i) Cola — pH 2.5	☐	☐	☐
ii) Pure water — pH 7	☐	☐	☐
iii) Beer — pH 4.5	☐	☐	☐

Q2 When pollutants enter a **lake** or **river** in large amounts they can alter the pH of the water.

Complete the passage below using the words provided, to describe how a change in the pH of a polluted lake could be reversed.

raise   acid   alkali   neutralisation   acidic   lower   oxidation

If a water sample taken from a lake is too ....,

then alkali needs be added to .... the pH.

However if the water sample is too alkaline then it is necessary to add

.... to the lake. This process is called

....

Top Tips: Acids aren't just the bottles of stuff that chemists keep in their store rooms, that can burn your face off. Loads of things in the real world are acidic — like lemon juice. And wine.

Acids and Alkalis

Q3 An industrial company is using **acids** and **alkalis** to make **salts**.

a) Tick the boxes to show which of the sentences below are **true** and which are **false**.

	True	False
i) All alkalis have a pH below 7.	☐	☐
ii) All acids have a pH above 7.	☐	☐
iii) A neutral substance has a pH of 7.	☐	☐
iv) Alkalis dissolve in water to give solutions.	☐	☐
v) Adding an alkali to an acid lowers its pH.	☐	☐

b) Complete the general word equation for **neutralisation**.

.... + ... → salt + ...

Q4 **Raw materials** from the earth can be used to manufacture useful **acids** and **bases**.

a) **i)** **Ammonia** is an base. What are the raw materials needed to make ammonia?

....

....

ii) The neutralisation reactions of ammonia produce **salts**.
Give **one** use for these salts.

....

b) **Sodium hydroxide** is also a base.

i) Give **one** raw material needed to make sodium hydroxide.

....

ii) State **where** the raw material you gave in part **i)** can be found.

....

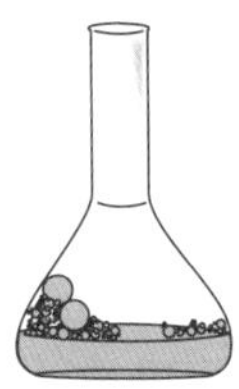
Acid

Base

c) What are the raw materials needed to make **sulfuric acid**?

....

Reactions of Acids

Q1 A chemist is using **acids** and **alkalis** to make **salts**.

Complete the following equations by choosing from the chemicals below.

zinc oxide	water	potassium sulfate
sodium nitrate	sulfuric acid	magnesium hydroxide

a) hydrochloric acid + copper(II) oxide → copper(II) chloride + ...

b) nitric acid + sodium hydroxide → .... + water

c) .... + magnesium oxide → magnesium sulfate + water

d) sulfuric acid + potassium hydroxide → .... + water

e) hydrochloric acid + ... → zinc chloride + water

f) nitric acid + ... → magnesium nitrate + water

Q2 Gita adds a small piece of **zinc** to a test tube containing **sulfuric acid**.

a) Describe what Gita will see.

....

b) Write a word equation for the reaction between zinc and sulfuric acid.

....

Q3 James is investigating some chemicals that are used as **food additives**.

a) First, James investigates **magnesium chloride**. Name the metal and acid that can be used to produce magnesium chloride.

Metal: ....

Acid: ....

b) James then researches **sodium chloride**. Write a word equation to show how sodium chloride could be prepared using a metal and an acid.

....

Reactions of Acids and Chemical Formulae

Q1 **Ammonium chloride** is a nitrogen-containing salt. It can be used to make fertilisers.

The word equation below shows how **ammonium chloride** can be made commercially. Complete the word equation using some of the words given.

.... acid + ... → ammonium chloride

nitric sulfuric hydrochloric ammonia hydrogen chlorine

Q2 A research scientist is developing a product to remove deposits of **calcium carbonate** (limescale) from kettles. She thinks that one way to get rid of it is to use a **dilute acid**. She tests this idea using **nitric acid**, **sulfuric acid** and **hydrochloric acid**.

Complete the word equations below to show the products that will be formed in these tests.

a) nitric acid + calcium carbonate

→ .... + ... + ...

b) sulfuric acid + calcium carbonate

→ .... + ... + ...

c) hydrochloric acid + calcium carbonate

→ .... + ... + ...

Q3 For each of the molecules shown below, give the **number** and **type** of each **atom** present. Use the table on the right to help you. The first one has been done for you.

Symbol	Atom
C	carbon
O	oxygen
H	hydrogen
Cl	chlorine
Mg	magnesium
Ca	calcium

CO_2

1 carbon atom, 2 oxygen atoms

a) **HCl**

....

b) **$MgCl_2$**

....

c) **$CaCO_3$**

....

Solutions

Q1 A teacher is making **sodium hydroxide solution** of a known **concentration** for an experiment. The instructions she is following include the terms **solute**, **solvent** and **solution**.

Draw lines to match up each of these terms with the correct example on the right.

solute	sodium hydroxide
solvent	water
solution	sodium hydroxide dissolved in water

Q2 Albert is making up **stock solutions** in his lab.

A stock solution is just a large volume of a chemical at a known concentration.

a) Albert dissolved **50 g** of lithium chloride in water to make **250 cm³** of solution. What is the **concentration**, in g/litre, of the lithium chloride solution he has made?

....

....

b) Albert then dissolved **40 g** of copper sulfate in water to make **2 litres** of solution. What is the **concentration**, in g/litre, of the copper sulfate solution he has made up?

....

....

c) Albert wants to make a **75 g/litre** solution of sodium hydroxide. What **mass** of sodium hydroxide pellets should Albert dissolve to make **20 litres** of solution?

....

....

Q3 Clive's job is to make up **solutions** to sell to laboratories and factories. He has been asked to make up an order of **4 litres of 50 g/litre copper chloride** solution.

a) Before handling the copper chloride, what should Clive do?

....

b) Describe the steps Clive should take to make up this order.

....

....

....

Solutions

Q4 It's George's job to make the chemical **solutions** for the science teachers in a school lab.

a) His first job is to make up 3 litres of sodium chloride solution with a **concentration of 10 g/litre**.

i) How much sodium chloride will it take to make up **one litre** of solution?

ii) Using your answer to part **i)**, how much sodium chloride does George need to make up **3 litres** of solution?

b) His next job is to make up **250 cm³** of magnesium sulfate solution at a **concentration of 8 g/litre**. How much magnesium sulfate will it take to make up 250 cm³ of solution?

c) The next teacher specified his order slightly differently. He wanted **2 litres** of copper chloride solution at a **concentration of 0.25 g/cm³**. How much copper chloride will it take to make up 2 litres of solution?

Remember: 1 litre = 1000 cm³

Q5 A student evaporated a **200 cm³** sample of sea water. He was left with 7 g of **sodium chloride**.

What was the concentration, in **g/cm³**, of sodium chloride in the sea water?

Q6 Naveena is working out how much **solid** she needs to make various **solutions**.

a) How many **grams** of magnesium chloride does she need to make 300 cm³ of a 0.5 g/cm³ solution?

b) How many **grams** of sodium carbonate does she need to make 4 litres of a 50 g/litre solution?

Making Insoluble Salts

Q1 Kamal is making some **insoluble salts** in his lab.

a) Kamal carries out a reaction that produces insoluble **calcium carbonate** and **sodium chloride** in solution. Which chemicals did he react together?
Tick **two** boxes.

- [ ] calcium chloride
- [ ] potassium chloride
- [ ] sodium carbonate
- [ ] sodium chloride
- [ ] calcium nitrate

Remember: the different bits of the reactants need to "swap partners".

b) Complete the **word** equations for the formation of **insoluble salts** when he mixes the following:

i) potassium phosphate + cobalt chloride

→ .... + ...

ii) magnesium nitrate + sodium carbonate

→ .... + ...

Q2 Ghassan needs to make **copper hydroxide**, using the following reaction:

copper sulfate +	sodium hydroxide →	copper hydroxide +	sodium sulfate
soluble	**soluble**	**insoluble**	**soluble**

a) Briefly describe the method Ghassan will use in his experiment.

....

....

b) What will Ghassan see when he mixes the copper sulfate and sodium hydroxide solutions together?

....

c) What is the name given to this type of reaction?
Tick **one** box.

- [ ] precipitation
- [ ] filtration
- [ ] neutralisation
- [ ] crystallisation

Top Tips: It's important that you get the method for making insoluble salts straight in your mind. It's pretty likely that you'll get asked something to do with these reactions, and those pesky word equations might show their faces. There's even more practice to be had on the next page. Lucky you.

Making Insoluble Salts

Q3 Gethin is a research chemist at a pigment factory. He carries out a precipitation reaction using two solutions to produce insoluble **copper(II) carbonate** and soluble **sodium nitrate**.

a) Write the **word equation** for the reaction that Gethin carried out.

....

b) Describe how Gethin should **separate** the **copper(II) carbonate** from the solution.

....

....

....

c) Why couldn't he use the same method to separate out **sodium nitrate**?

....

....

Q4 Keira is researching **lead iodide**, which can be used as a detector material for X-rays. She makes some **insoluble** lead iodide by mixing **lead nitrate** and **sodium iodide** and then **filters** the product and obtains a **filtrate** and a **residue**.

a) What is meant by the term **filtrate**?

....

b) What is meant by the term **residue**?

....

c) After filtering the product, Keira rinses and dries the lead iodide.

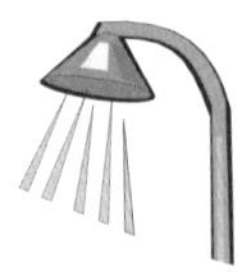

i) Why does the solid need to be rinsed?

....

ii) Why is it important to use distilled water and not just tap water to rinse the solid?

....

iii) Describe how the solid could be **dried** after rinsing.

....

Making Soluble Salts

Q1 Bob is making a sample of **magnesium sulfate** crystals. Magnesium sulfate is **soluble** and is made from **magnesium oxide** and **sulfuric acid**.

a) Write a **word** equation for the reaction.

....

b) Use the words in the box to complete the passage below.

filtration	magnesium oxide	heating	acid	filtrate
distillation	stirring	sterilisation	residue	evaporation

Bob slowly adds the magnesium oxide powder to the acid, ... the mixture as he does so. He knows that all the .... has reacted when he sees bits of powder at the bottom of the beaker. Bob then gets rid of the powder by .... Next, Bob removes the magnesium sulfate from the .... by ....

c) Bob wants to make the magnesium sulfate crystals quite **quickly**.
The sentences below describe how he should do this, but they are in the wrong order.

Number the boxes to show the correct order.

☐ **Put the solution in an evaporating basin.**

☐ **Scrape the residue out of the basin.**

☐ **Apply gentle heat with a Bunsen burner.**

☐ **Place the evaporating basin on a tripod and gauze.**

Bob wanted the crystals quickly.

d) Describe how Bob could change his method if he wanted to produce **larger crystals**.

....

....

e) What **safety precautions** should be taken during this procedure?

....

....

f) Give **one** use for magnesium sulfate.

....

Making Soluble Salts

Q2 A chemistry class is reading through a method for making a **soluble salt**. They comes across the words **crystallisation**, **evaporation** and **residue**.

Draw lines to match each word with its correct description.

crystallisation	the substance left in a container after another has been removed
evaporation	the formation of solid particles from a solution
residue	the conversion of water from a liquid to a gas

Q3 Janine wants to make an exact amount of **soluble copper chloride** by adding **insoluble copper oxide** to **hydrochloric acid**.

a) Write a **word** equation for this reaction.

....

b) Janine only needs to measure out **one** of the chemicals accurately.

i) Which chemical would she need to measure out accurately? Give a reason for your answer.

....

....

ii) Which **apparatus** would you suggest she used to measure out this chemical?

....

Q4 Bashira is making some **soluble salts** in the lab.

Write **word** equations for the reactions that occur when she mixes:

a) hydrochloric acid and sodium hydroxide

....

b) sulfuric acid and potassium hydroxide

....

Top Tips: You might not find making salts the most thrilling of topics, but it is important that you know about how to make a soluble salt and then separate it from solution. You can't use the same techniques that you would for insoluble salts — so make sure you learn the different processes.

Neutralising an Acid

Q1 **Sodium sulfate** can be made by reacting **sodium hydroxide** (an alkali) with **sulfuric acid**.

sulfuric acid + sodium hydroxide → sodium sulfate + water

a) **i)** The alkali is added gradually to the acid. What happens to the **pH** of the reaction mixture as the alkali is added?

....

ii) The pH of the reaction mixture can be measured using a **pH meter**. How else could the pH be measured?

....

b) Fill in the gaps to complete the sentence.

When the pH reaches exactly .... the reaction is complete.

The acid and alkali have .... each other.

c) Once the reaction is complete, how are crystals of sodium sulfate obtained from the solution?

....

Q2 Chemists often draw **graphs** to represent how the **pH** of a mixture changes during a titration. The graph below shows how the pH changes when **sulfuric acid** is added to **sodium hydroxide** solution.

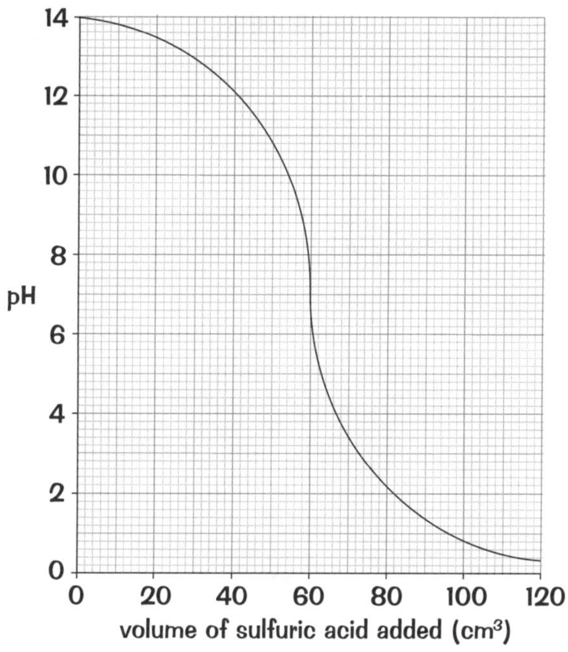

a) What was the pH of the sodium hydroxide solution **before** the titration?

....

b) How much sulfuric acid was needed to **neutralise** the alkali?

....

c) On the graph, sketch how the pH would change if alkali was being added to acid.

For part c), think about what the pH would be at the start and how it would change as you added the alkali.

Chemical Synthesis and Yields

Q1 **Ethene** is used to make the world's biggest selling plastic — **polyethene**. The diagram below shows two **industrial reaction schemes** to make ethene.

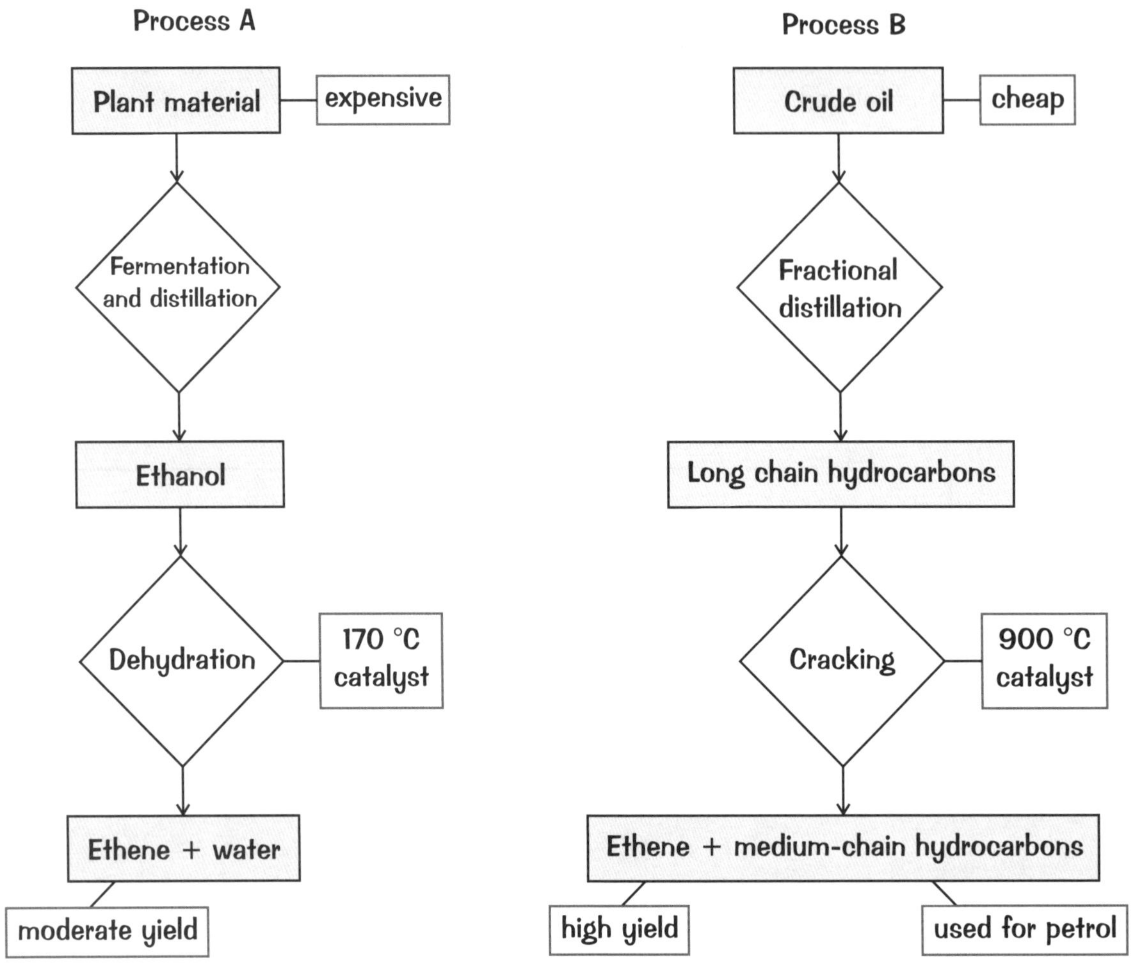

a) Ethene is mainly produced using **process B**. Suggest **two** reasons for this.

....

....

b) Suggest **two** reasons why process A might become **more popular** in the future.

....

....

....

c) Which process produces **more waste**? Explain your answer.

....

....

Chemical Synthesis and Yields

Q2 Aaliya is a research chemist in the **chemical industry**. She is carrying out an experiment to work out the **percentage yield** from a particular reaction. She mixes barium chloride and sodium sulfate solutions in a beaker. **Insoluble** barium sulfate was formed.

a) Complete the following paragraph using the words provided.

percentage yield	yield	predicted

The amount of product you get from a reaction is known as the ....

The .... compares how much product you actually get to the amount you ....

b) Aaliya calculated that she should produce a yield of **15 g** of barium sulfate. However, after completing the experiment she found she had only obtained **6 g**.

Calculate the **percentage yield** for this reaction.

$$\% \text{ yield} = \frac{\text{yield}}{\text{theoretical yield}} \times 100$$

....

....

Q3 Timothy, a **research chemist**, is investigating three different **methods** of producing hydrochloric acid. His results are shown in the table below.

Method	Theoretical yield (kg)	Actual yield (kg)	Percentage yield
A	56	23.5	
B	84	38	
C	28	17	

a) i) Fill in the table by calculating the percentage yield of each method.

ii) Based on the information in the table, which method would Timothy be most interested in? ....

b) Suggest **two** other factors Timothy would consider when choosing a method to use on a **large scale**.

1. ....

2. ....

Rates of Reaction

Q1 Mike works for a **pharmaceutical company**. His job is to **refine** the chemical processes the company uses to increase **profitability**. This often involves maximising the **rate of a reaction**.

a) Which of the following statements correctly define the term 'rate of a chemical reaction'? Tick **two** boxes.

The amount of precipitate that is formed. ☐

The amount of product formed divided by the time taken. ☐

How fast the reactants are changed into products. ☐

How quickly the reactants mix together. ☐

b) Mike is currently working on the reaction:

aluminium (s) **+ hydrochloric acid** (aq) → **hydrogen** (g) **+ aluminium trichloride** (aq)

Complete the diagram below to show how Mike could measure the rate of this reaction.

Look at the state symbols of the products.

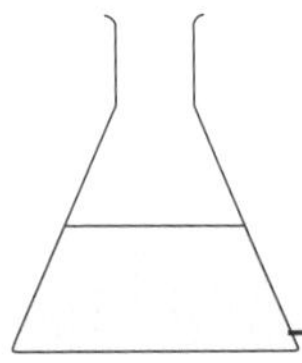

Q2 Ralph is investigating how the **rate of a reaction** depends on the **concentration** of acid he uses. Ralph measures the **volume of gas** produced in **20 seconds** using three different concentrations of acid. His results are shown below.

Reaction	1	2	3
Volume of gas produced (cm^3)	80	200	40
Rate (cm^3/s)	4		

a) Complete the table with the rates of the second two reactions.

Rate = $\frac{\text{amount of product}}{\text{time}}$

b) In which reaction did Ralph use the **most concentrated acid**? Explain your answer.

....

....

c) Ralph repeated reaction 1 using a **catalyst**. What effect would this have on the volume of gas produced in 20 seconds? Circle the correct answer.

increase it no change decrease it

Rates of Reaction

Q3 **Silver nitrate** is used in **photographic imaging**. It is made by reacting silver with nitric acid.

silver (s) + nitric acid (aq) → silver nitrate (aq) + nitric oxide (g) + water (l)

The graph below shows how the mass of a reaction batch changed as the reaction progressed.

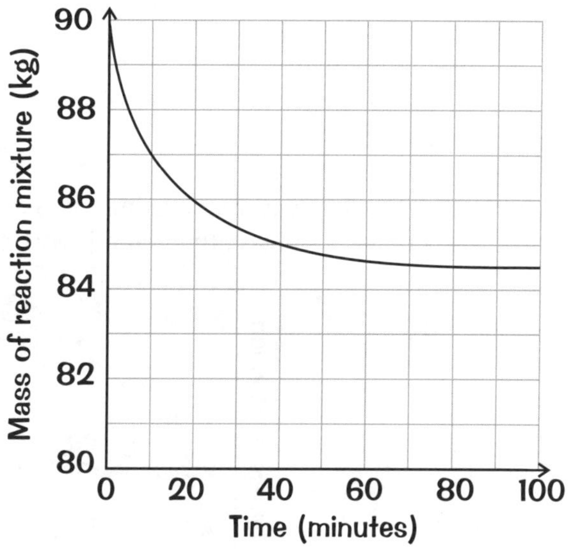

a) What mass of reactants was **lost** in the first **10 minutes** of the reaction?

....

b) How long did it take for the reaction mixture to lose **5 kg**?

....

c) Why does the mass of the reaction mixture **decrease** as the reaction proceeds?

....

....

d) Manufacturers of silver nitrate control the rate of the reaction to make sure it is profitable. Suggest **two** ways to speed up the reaction.

1. ....

2. ....

Q4 Use some of the words provided to complete the sentences below about measuring rates of reaction.

faster	speed	volume	reactants	gas	mass	formed	precipitation

In a .... reaction you usually measure how quickly the product is formed. The product turns the solution cloudy. The .... it turns cloudy the quicker the reaction. In a reaction that produces a .... you can measure how quickly the .... of the reactants changes or measure the .... of gas given off in a certain time interval.

Top Tips: If you can't read graphs and tables, you'll struggle with questions about rates of reactions. Never fear though — all it takes is practice and you'll be an expert. Bored, but an expert.

Rates of Reaction

Q5 **Barium sulfate** is used as a white pigment in **paints**. It can be made inside a fume cupboard using the reaction shown below.

barium chloride(aq) + sulfuric acid(aq) → barium sulfate(s) + hydrochloric acid(aq)

a) Describe a method that could be used to **monitor** the rate of this reaction.

....

....

One of the products is a solid — the reactants are both solutions.

b) Barium sulfate was made using the reaction above, under four different sets of conditions. The curves A to D on the graph below show the rates of the four reactions.

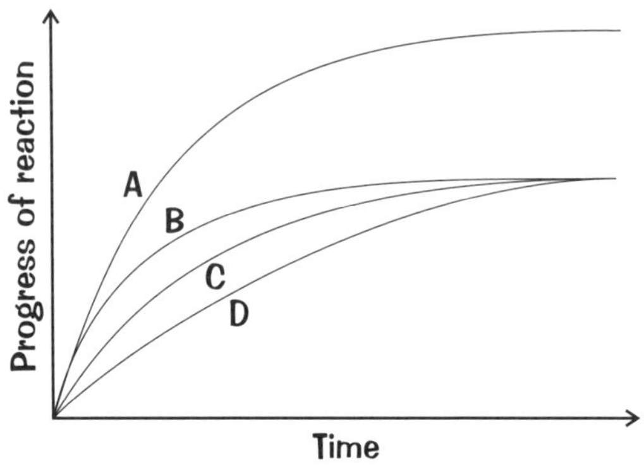

Draw lines to match the conditions described below with the curves on the graph.

room temperature	A
high temperature with a catalyst and increased amounts of barium chloride and sulfuric acid	B
high temperature	C
high temperature with a catalyst	D

c) What is meant by the term '**catalyst**'?

....

Q6 **Coal** is used as a **fuel** in power stations and people's homes. When it burns, a **chemical reaction** called **combustion** is taking place.

In a power station, the coal is ground up into a fine powder. In the home, coal is used in lumps. How will the **size** of the pieces of coal used affect the rate of combustion?

....

....

Mixtures

Q1 Mayonnaise is made by blending together vegetable oil and egg yolk to form an **emulsion**.

a) What is an emulsion?

....

b) What will happen to an emulsion of egg yolk and oil if it is left for a few days?

....

....

c) Mayonnaise contains an emulsifier. Why are **emulsifiers** added to emulsions? Tick **one** box.

☐ To change the colour of the emulsion.

☐ So that the two liquids in the emulsion both dissolve in each other.

☐ To help the two liquids in the emulsion mix together and stop them from separating out.

☐ So that the emulsion is safe to use.

d) Name **two** other household products that are emulsions.

1. ....

2. ....

Q2 Lots of everyday products are **emulsions**, e.g. some food products and drinks.

a) Tick the boxes to show which of the sentences below are **true** or **false**.

	True	False
i) Emulsions are all edible.	☐	☐
ii) Ice cream is an example of an emulsion.	☐	☐
iii) Emulsions are always cloudy.	☐	☐
iv) In an emulsion one component dissolves in another.	☐	☐

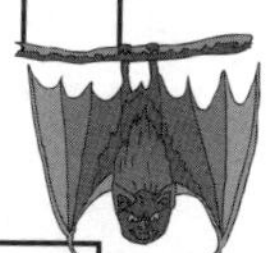

b) Complete the sentences below by circling the correct word(s) in the pair.

i) Emulsions are made by **slowly** / **quickly** adding two liquids together whilst beating the mixture continuously.

ii) Emulsions are useful because their properties are **different from** / **the same as** the properties of their ingredients.

Mixtures

Q3 **Calamine lotion** is a popular treatment for skin irritation.
It is a **suspension** of calamine powder in **water**.

a) Complete the passage about suspensions using some of the words from the list.

do	liquid	don't	small	gas	suspend	dissolve

A suspension is a mixture of .... solid particles mixed in with a .... The particles .... mix completely — they don't .... and there are no chemical bonds.

b) Explain why a bottle of calamine lotion gets a clear layer on top if it's left standing for a few weeks.

....

....

c) Give **two** other examples of a suspension.

1. ....

2. ....

Q4 Harold creates a **suspension** in a jar by mixing silt with water. Complete the diagrams below by drawing **silt particles** to show the **suspension**, and also to show what will have happened inside the jar a **few hours later**.

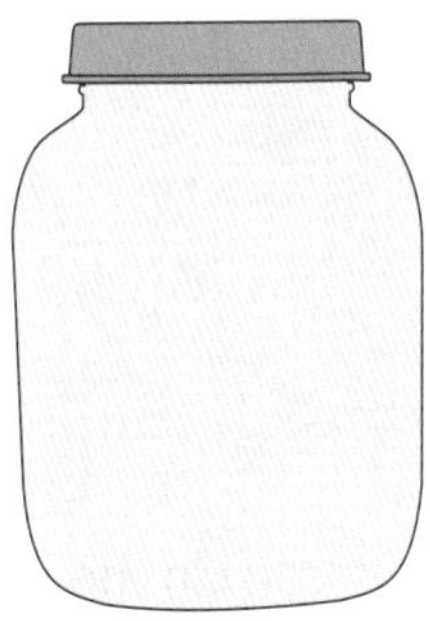

Initial suspension

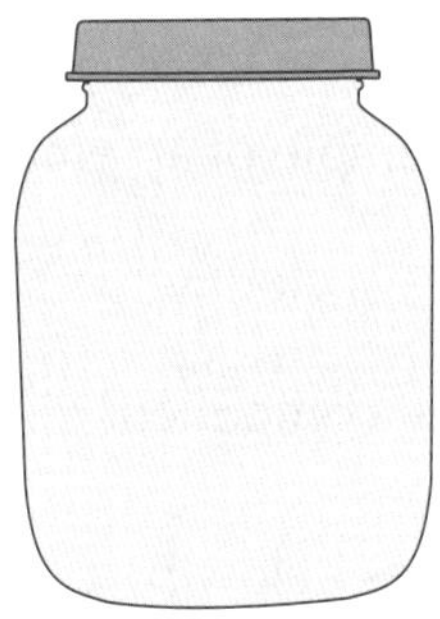

After a few hours

Top Tips: Emulsions, suspensions, mayonnaise — another batch of technical words to add to your brain. Actually, maybe mayonnaise isn't a technical word, just a hero of the sandwich world. Make sure you can describe what emulsions and suspensions are. You also need to be able to give examples of both too. Anyhow, I won't keep you in suspension any longer, here's the next page....

Testing Formulations

Q1 The table below shows the results of a **quality control** test at **Pete's Paints**.

	Ideal paint	Batch A	Batch B	Batch C
Binder	40	30	41	45
Pigment	10	10	9	5
Solvent	50	60	50	50

a) Which of the batches is closest to the ideal composition? ....

b) The binder is used to hold the pigment particles together. The pigment particles control the paint colour. The amount of solvent controls the thickness of the paint — the more solvent there is, the thinner the paint.

i) Which batch of paint will probably be too runny? ....

ii) Which batch of paint will not be the right colour? ....

c) Give **two** reasons why companies test their products before they go on sale.

1. ....

2. ....

Q2 Ails Away is developing a new **flu remedy**. They test three formulations on groups of **volunteers**. Each person fills in a **questionnaire** rating how well the remedy eased their **symptoms**.

The table below shows the average scores for each remedy tested. Scores go from 0 to 5, with 0 being no change and 5 meaning the symptoms disappeared completely.

Symptom	Remedy A	Remedy B	Remedy C
Blocked nose	2	3	4
Sinus pain	1	4	3
Headaches	1	4	4

a) Which formulation(s) should the company continue to develop? **A** **B** **C**

b) Suggest **one** other thing the formulations would need to be tested for before they went on sale.

....

c) Before the remedy went on sale it would be tested to ensure it met the national standards. Why is it important to have national standards for products like this?

....

Mixed Questions — Unit 2: Topic 4

Q1 **Nitric acid** is used in the manufacture of **fertilisers** and **explosives**.

a) Nitric acid will **corrode** living tissue. Circle the correct hazard symbol for nitric acid.

b) What reading would **nitric acid** give on a pH meter? Circle the correct answer.

1-2 **6.5-7.5** **12-13**

c) The equipment shown below is used to react sodium hydroxide with nitric acid.

i) Name the pieces of equipment labelled on the diagram.

A ....

B ....

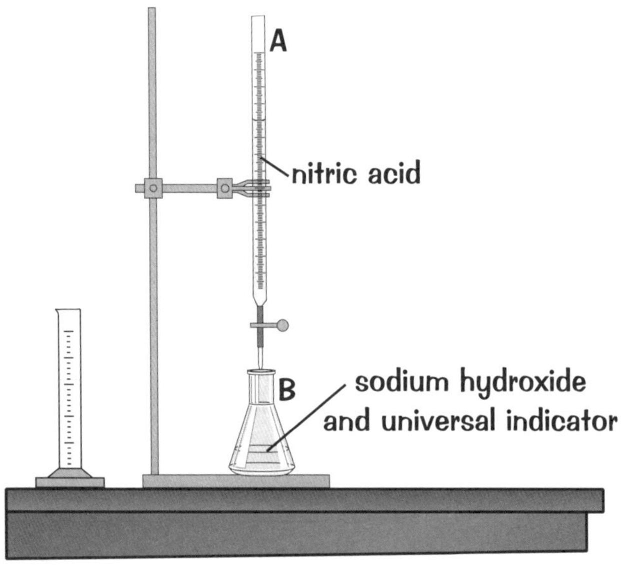

ii) What type of reaction is taking place?

....

iii) What will be the **pH** of the solution when the reaction is complete?

....

iv) Describe how the reaction could be **monitored** to show when it is complete.

....

....

v) What are the **products** of the reaction?

....

d) Complete the following word equations.

i) nitric acid + zinc → ....

ii) nitric acid + magnesium carbonate → ....

iii) nitric acid + copper(II) oxide → ....

Mixed Questions — Unit 2: Topic 4

Q2 **Copper chloride** can be prepared by mixing copper oxide and hydrochloric acid, as shown in steps A and B below, then following the further steps C and D.

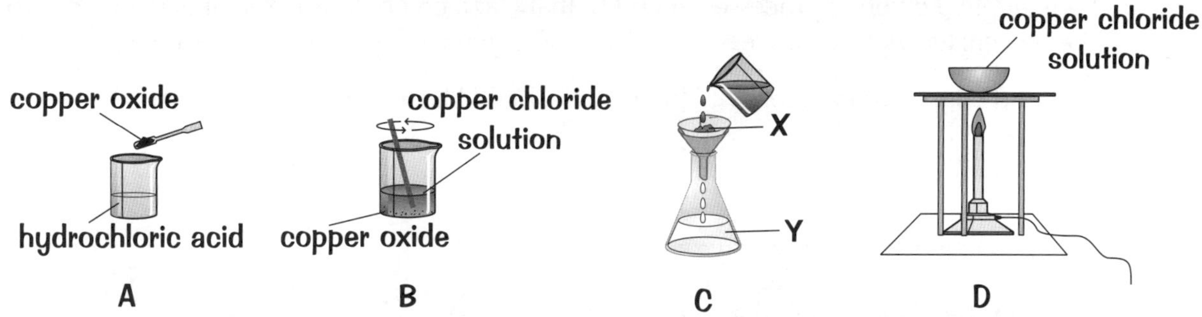

Copper oxide is a black, **insoluble solid**. Copper chloride solution is a **blue liquid**.

a) How can you be sure that all the hydrochloric acid has reacted?

....

b) Look at process C. Which of the labels (X or Y) is pointing to:

i) the **filtrate**? .... **ii)** the insoluble residue? ....

c) **i)** Describe how crystals of copper chloride are obtained in process D.

....

ii) How could **larger** crystals of copper chloride be obtained?

....

The graph below shows the concentration of copper chloride solution as the reaction progresses.

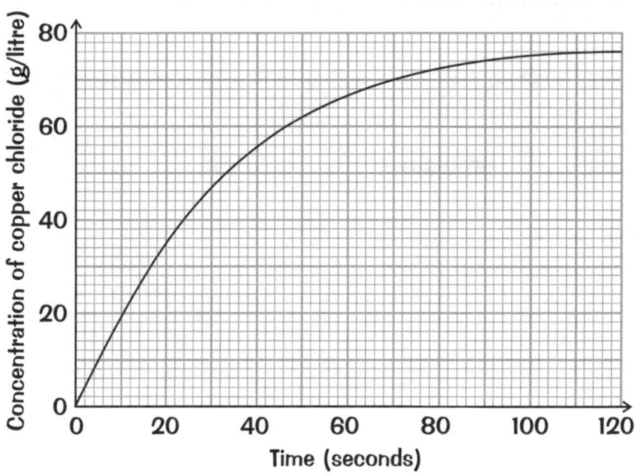

d) What is the concentration of copper chloride solution after 50 seconds?

....

e) How long does it take for the concentration to reach 40 g/litre?

....

f) What is the final concentration of copper chloride solution?

....

g) Give **two** ways in which the rate of the reaction could be increased.

1. ....

2. ....

Mixed Questions — Unit 2: Topic 4

Q3 Hazleen is developing a form of the painkiller **ibuprofen** that can be given to **children**.

a) There are two different processes, A and B, that Hazleen could use to manufacture ibuprofen. The percentage yield of process A is 40%. The percentage yield of process B is 77%.

i) Based on this information, which process should Hazleen use? Explain your answer.

....

....

ii) Give **three** things, other than yield, that Hazleen should consider when choosing which process to use.

1. ....

2. ....

3. ....

b) The chemical formula for ibuprofen is $\mathbf{C_{13}H_{18}O_2}$.

C = carbon, H = hydrogen and O = oxygen.

List the number of atoms of each type in a molecule of ibuprofen.

....

c) Ibuprofen is a '**fine**' chemical. Explain what this means.

....

d) Hazleen's final product consists of solid particles of ibuprofen dispersed in a syrupy liquid. What type of mixture is this? Circle the correct answer.

extrusion **suspension** **emulsion** **solution**

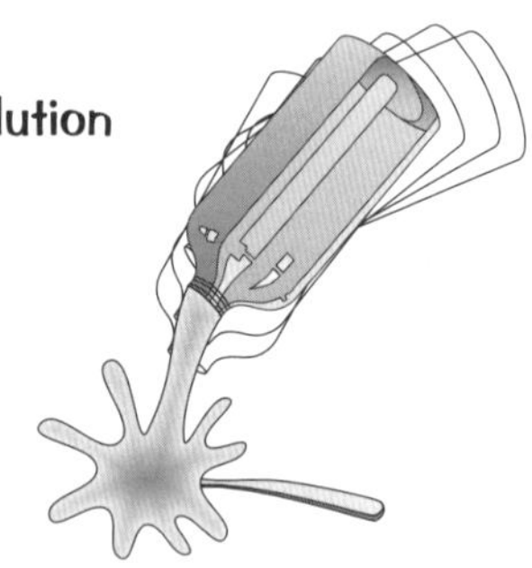

e) The concentration of ibuprofen in the product is 20 g/litre. Calculate the mass of ibuprofen contained in a 2.5 ml dose.

....

....

....

f) The product will undergo a series of tests before it is allowed to go on sale. Give **two** reasons why it will be tested.

1. ....

2. ....